Sunlight and Shadows

by

Douglas A. Cox

Sunlight and Shadows
Douglas A. Cox
1000 N. Green Valley Parkway
Suite 440-392
Henderson, NV 89074
United States of America
www.DougCoxOnline.com
Email: Doug@DougCoxOnline.com

Editing by Sharon Norman
Book Layout & Design by Linda A. Bell
www.HearttoHeartStudio.com

© 2020 Douglas A. Cox - All Rights Reserved

No part of this book may be reproduced or transmitted in any form or by any means, electronic or mechanical, including photocopying, recording or by any information storage and retrieval system without written permission from the author.

BIOGRAPHY & AUTOBIOGRAPHY/personal memoirs/sunlight and shadows/Douglas A. Cox -1st. ed.

ISBN: 9798663734363

Printed in the United States of America

Disclaimer
The purpose of this book is to educate, motivate, and inspire. The author shall have neither liability nor responsibility to any person or entity with respect to any loss or damage caused or alleged to be caused directly or indirectly by the information contained in this book.

CONTENTS

In the Beginning 7
A Blind Man's Movie 10
A Love Story 12
Feathers 14
Humming 16
Walden 18
The Falcon 20
Landing 22
Corn Dog 24
The Time Machine 26
Talk 28
Calico Ghost Town 30
The City 32
Hollister 34
Valley Forge 36
Wabi Sabi 38
Treasure 40
Where You Been? 42
Educare (Ed-you-car-eh) 44
Baseline 46
Big Box Day 48
Change 50
Le Rêve 52
Meadowlark 54
Whaleshead 56
Harvest Moon 58
Wham! 60
Lost! 62
Magic Leaves 64
Darkness 66
The Ride 68
Shadows 70

Different	72
Song-Dog	74
Four Jacks	76
Sweet Freedom	78
White Bird	80
Tween	82
Curious?	84
The Instrument	86
The Key	88
If It's Tuesday	90
Hugs	92
The Timekeeper (Lichen)	94
The Web	96
Sunlight	98
Lead	100
Flight #565	102
Dialect	104
Frantic (Part One)	106
Frantic (Part Two...)	108
Grandpa's Kite	110
Circle of Concern	112
Bloom	114
Burbank	116
Coach	118
Solid Gold	120
Furry and Feathered Family	122
Honest	124
Changing of the Guard	126
Making the Grade	128
Friends	130
"A"	132
Hero (RIP Papa)	134
A Gift (Packages)	136
Sentinel Species	138
Let's Ride	140
Ruby Rapidamente	142

Windows	144
Coyote	146
Wings	148
"Cool"	150
The Flame	152
Kindness	154
The Bowl	156
Up!	158
Heart Work	160
The Young Professors	162
Meow!	164
Misty	166
Mosskins	168
History and Magic	170
My Desk	172
Mystery	174
New Growth	176
The Night Sky	178
Pirates	180
Prestidigitator	182
Rest	184
Reverence Lost	186
Sage	188
Say Yes!	190
Desert Shrimp	192
Seabird	194
Skies	196
Hear Hear	198
Sentinel	200
A Moment	202
The Jersey	204
Sky Dance	206
Fragrance	208
His Desk	210
First Song	212
Where or When	214

Reminiscence of a Sweet Surprise (Part One) 216
Reminiscence of a Sweet Surprise (Part Two) 218

Reader's Favorites: Thoughts that Rhyme at Holiday Time!

Winter | Alaskan Night 221
New Year's Eve | Breaking the Glass 222
The Paper 223
Valentine's Day | The Valentine 224
I Love You More 225
St. Patrick's Day | Hiding Place 226
Little Men 227
The Circle 228
May Day | Aloha 229
Mother's Day | Mom and Me 230
My Mother's Eyes 231
Memorial Day | Spirit Light and Fireflies 232
Transferring the Flag 233
Summer | Butterfly Shadows 234
Flag Day | Glory 235
Father's Day | The Living Years 236
Independence Day | Words 237
Ride the Lightning 238
Autumn | Memories 239
Labor Day | Work 240
Lights Across a Field 241
A Jack-O-Lantern Moon 242
Halloween | Fright Night 243
Secret Soldiers 244
Veteran's Day | The Reason 245
Thanksgiving | Homecoming 246
Thanks Giving 247
Beneath a Christmas Sky 248
Lost and Found 249
Christmas | Timeless 250

In the Beginning

In the wonderful film, *Big Wednesday,* the narrator asks the profound question, *"Where does the wind come from?"* In that same spirit, our dear friend, Dottie, asked me, *"Where did you come from?"* Dottie, who is a bright ninety-seven years young, had been reading one of my books and was inspired to try to figure me out. In her beautiful rich voice, which arrives and departs like the wind, she asked, *"How did you get to be like this?"* She assured me that it was a positive inquiry. Her question caused me to think about my arrival, where I came from and most importantly, how I came to be as I am.

My answer, as perhaps it will be in your life, springs forth from people. Physically, financially, emotionally and spiritually, we become the sum total and production of the experiences shared with and about our families, our friends and our acquaintances. Here are a handful of hints that will help you come to know your author.

Born as I was in Hollywood California during world war two, we raised nearly all of the food served at our dining table. Physically, my little growing body received the gift of fresh fruit, vegetables, and dairy products; all chemical free. From the earliest days of my memory, my brother and I were responsible for the chicken and rabbit our mother prepared for our meals. More than once, a hungry neighbor would come to our home for a visit. Too proud to ask, they would sit in our kitchen until Mom insisted that they take home a care package from our victory garden.

Our immediate family was a marvelous patchwork quilt in itself. Our mother, a marvelous, promiscuous alcoholic, was a beautiful, brilliant conversationalist, vocalist, and raconteur. That explains the fact that my sibs and I each boast of a different father. Our dad, though not biological, was a treasure of a man. Charlie was a teetotaler and wizard of the municipal bond world. He was gentle of hand and word and a constant inspiration. My brother, seven years my senior, was and is my hero. Although we were too far apart for much play and interaction, he always made time to chat, share and then tell me to bug off. He brought to our dinner table, where we gathered every evening to dine, discuss and sing together, his growing intellect and penchant for using our beautiful English language properly and eloquently.

Our sister, seven years younger, who became a brilliant musicologist and vocalist, was my confidant. We were partners in crime. I always believed that I was her knight-in-shining-armor and have always been overjoyed to discover that she remembers this as well. The best relationships always include make believe so we named the ancient eucalyptus trees under which we played "The Cramellos!" She and I created our own fun and our own language.

My parent's friends truly covered the waterfront in both their celebrations and beliefs, and I was fascinated observing them. Having been raised color-blind I saw no races, colors, or creeds. These folks ranged from what one might describe as a little to the left of Karl Marx to the opposite side, way to the right of Genghis Khan. There were religious zealots, agnostics, and outright atheists. Most of our acquaintances, whatever their persuasions, were deeply passionate about their beliefs. I loved the fact that Mom and Dad always allowed us to explore the experience and rarely told us what we should believe. We made up our own minds and here we are.

In response to my last book, *Mind Movies,* my readers commented that the joy of it was being able to pick up the book anytime of the day or night, open to any page and be entertained and enlightened for as long as they chose. So, when I listened to my friend Jesse Collin Young singing *"Get Together"* and heard him profess, *"We are but a moment's sunlight fading in the grass,"* I knew that I wanted to share these moments with you.

Now, as we head into what will become our new normal, I am heading back out into this world of *Sunlight and Shadows*. Will you join me...

Tigger

A Blind Man's Movie

Our kit-cat stands meowing in the kitchen... She is pretending to be hungry. We both know that once served, she will turn up her nose at the freshly presented food. The best part is when the can is first opened, the beggar will raise her nose in the air and sniff thoroughly, as the full food dish is carried from the sink to its presentation. She is making, *A Blind Man's Movie.*

When I worked with the Smothers Brothers, I met the most wonderful array of people. Among them was the RCA recording artist, writer and brilliant comedian, Murray Roman. We had gotten together to celebrate the release of Murray's LP, *A Blind Man's Movie...* I loved the title, because it reminded me of so many true-life adventures that proved the truth of the expression. Example: It is pitch black at five a.m. on Doug's Mountain. On my way up in the darkness, I can smell the fragrance of Blue Catmint and Spires Russian Sage. A pre-dawn breath of air carries to me a hint of Raspberry Delight, Bush Sage and Glow Globe Thistle. Though I cannot see it, I am aware that I am surrounded by Creosote, California Juniper, Apricot Mallow, and Desert Golden Poppy. *A Blind Man's Movie* indeed!

On my way down, I am reminded that the soundtrack is also of great importance in *A Blind Man's Movie.* Just as the call of the poorwills starts to fade, the voices of the Gambel's Quail begin their outreach and a late returning coyote howls at me, to get home and get the coffee going.

Wherever you live, step outside, stand still or sit, close your eyes and just listen to the Academy Award presentation of your own *Blind Man's Movie*... Do it now. Our beloved friend Murray Roman was killed in a tragic traffic accident shortly after the release of his LP.

The theater of the mind is a wondrous place...
Tigger

A Love Story

Whatever dance style, from the forties to the nineties, these two could do it. You pick the music; they were knocking it out of the park. I don't know about you, but I truly celebrate people in love and having fun.

My wife and I are dancers too. I'll bet you know that. We really love to kick up our heels and given the chance to do so with our neighbors, we jump at the opportunity. You find a holiday on the calendar and we can plan a dance around it. We recently did just that to celebrate the Fourth of July. What fun! Great Deejay, great music and plenty of energy and laughter.

We shared the party with some dear friends who moved here from California. When the evening was coming to a close, they opened up the conversation by saying, *"You guys were cutting it up out there. That dance floor was sawdust!"* My response was, *"You two are the only California Cruisers that can out-dance us!"* My friend's reply was priceless. *"My wife sweeps my heart away. The dance floor gives the opportunity for love in motion."* Then he concluded by saying, *"Living the dream, dancing with my sweetheart! Doesn't get much better than that!"*

Take a moment to let those words sink in. Most of the folks I know wouldn't confess the depth of their affection for their spouse in private, let alone in public. Why is that? We are either missing that romantic gene or we just don't care for our partner the way we once did, could or should.

How long has it been since you tried the surfer stomp, electric slide, fox trot, twist, monkey, west coast swing or plain old high school slow dance? You remember, trying to pump oil out of the ground by rocking side to side until your date needed Dramamine!

I once recorded a CD, *The Secrets of the Dance*. It was the exposé of my learning how to dance and the joy that I found in giving up old fears to share the secrets of the dance. Obviously, our friends had not only discovered the secrets but discovered the power of romance as inspiration.

Please save me a dance...
Tigger

Feathers

I love writing about experiences, places and things we hold in common. At age three, the ground is much closer to a wandering child than it will be when they are big and grown. That was how, on a magic backyard morning, in the foothills of California, I found my first feather. There in the moist green grass, was the bequest of a gray mourning dove. I felt like an explorer coming upon some unexpected treasure. I stooped to pick it up. As I ran my little fingers along the edge of this miracle of flight, I was fascinated! The textures and colors were a wonder to my young eyes. This was the first of my feather-treasure collection.

Underneath the huge live oak outside our kitchen window at Fox Ridges, I found my first blue jay feather. Standing beneath the giant branches, I was sure that I would never see anything more beautiful. The shades of blue and gray were so regal looking. Even as a child, I was aware of the majesty of this beautiful piece of art. The thought that this fragile blue treasure had flown above me in the sky, was a wonder. My collection was growing.

It was on a chilly autumn afternoon that this five-year-old prospector looked down on our gravel path, to see what appeared to be a bright orange shaft. The closer I got, the clearer it became, that I had come upon one of the most beautiful feathers in my collection. It was a flicker feather and a real beauty. Since those early days, my kids and now my grand and great grand kids have set out on search parties, in the hope of finding one of these treasures. Flickers are members of the woodpecker family. We find them by listening for their distinctive single note descending call. You will know when you spy one, by the illusion of a flickering flame in the sky just overhead.

My collection is now blessed with shafts of wonder, from Steve Irwin's Australia Zoo to Nanook's gift of feathers from Alaska...

Tigger

Humming

Thirty-Three-Million-Miles away, Mars is humming. It's true. The instrumentation that measures the activity of the red planet, confirms it. Mars is continually active, and its motion and ballet create the humming sound of a symphony, to the geniuses that monitor our curious neighbor.

Back here on earth, there is humming too. Being a happy and hopeless romantic, I recently cued up one of my favorite films, popped some corn and turned on Annette Benning and Warren Beatty in *Love Affair*. In the middle of this fine, romantic movie, there is a scene where, aircraft grounded, A.B. has tagged along with W.B. on a motorbike side trip to meet his aunt, Ms. Hepburn, at her home in Tahiti. It is immediately obvious that the two women find a solid connection and the star power is a pleasure to observe.

At one point, Ms. Hepburn crosses her sitting room, looks out across the pastureland and away to the lush green mountains, sits down at her beautiful grand piano and starts to play. Magnetized by the music, Annette comes forward, leans on the piano and begins to hum the beautiful love theme from the film. It is one of the most haunting and lovely compositions of Ennio Morricone. It is simply titled, "Love Affair," (piano solo). It goes straight to my heart.

Do you hum? If your answer is yes, good *on* you. If your answer is no, may I ask why not? Those of you who follow our Cox saga, have come to understand that much of our life was not easy. One of the things that made the tough times a bit more bearable, was the fact that we hummed. My mother had a beautiful voice and when the turbulence increased, her sweet tones were like honey on warm toast. I am happy to say that I inherited that habit and passed it on to my offspring. We call it *heart music*.

Tigger

Walden

Have you ever visited Concord, Massachusetts? Thanksgiving Season is a perfect time to wander through some very intriguing history: The Sleepy Hollow Cemetery, Luisa May Alcott Orchard House, the Old Manse, and the North Bridge, where the "shot heard round the world" was fired. After a fine luncheon in the Old Concord Inn, everything you see and everywhere you wander, will present you with a significant piece of history. Jack-O-Lanterns on porches, corn stalks in fields, fragrant apple baskets in wagons, and did I mention Walden Pond?

Right here, in the cradle of liberty, Walden Pond, this kettle hole formed by glaciers, ten to twelve thousand years ago, became the retreat and place of inspiration for Henry David Thoreau. I am inspired to write about my wanderings in the footsteps of the famous naturalist and author, because he often pointed out ways of seeing life and living, differently.

Scientists have just revealed the discovery of a new planet, that might become a possible target for human colonization. Thoreau, from the dining room of the Inn, often suggested we not buy a new coat, until we had distinguished ourselves in our old one. Seems to me, it would make sense to do the same with planets and worlds.

This wonderful blue marble that we call home, is in rough shape just now and it is not getting better. At some point in the future, if we are going to leave this earth for a new one, I would like to leave it better than it was when we inherited it! My friend Ray Charles said that our spirit lights up a room after we depart. Wouldn't it be beautiful, should it be written in the book of the universe, that we, homo sapiens, left this place better than the way in which we found it?

Count me in...
Tigger

The Falcon

My wife enjoys watching Good Morning America. This morning, as I headed out to our patio for breakfast, I passed the television and was stopped in my tracks. There she was, on the screen, *The Millennium Falcon,* bold as brass and full size. My heart skipped a beat. Robin Roberts and Michael Strahan had obviously set their weapons for stun and it worked...I was.

Many moons ago, on a late Christmas Eve, I checked to make certain that our youngest was sound asleep. I found him deep in dreamland. It was a perfect time to pull that secret box out of my closet. Thus began, one of the longest nights of my life. From Santa Barbara sunset to sunrise, I poured my heart and soul into constructing the very first model of the illustrious Falcon. I don't care what the box said, there were at least seven-million pieces and scout master be damned, it took all my attention and crafting skills, to make sure that Christmas morning held a bit of *Star Wars* Magic for our son.

"You've never heard of the Millennium Falcon? It's the ship that made the Kessel Run in less than twelve parsecs..." (Han Solo)

Talk about staying power and popularity... Forty-plus years after its introduction to our movie hungry world, *Star Wars: Galaxy's Edge,* opened in Disneyland California. *"Judge me by my size do you... And well you should not!"* Thank you, Master Yoda, and all of the Star Wars characters, who gave us a peek into a valiant and heroic way of living and being, in a very cynical world. *"May the force be with you!"*

One more incarnation: now we have the SpaceX Falcon 9 spacecraft, named in honor of the Millennium Falcon. It is a real life two stage-to-orbit medium lift vehicle that carried two of our NASA astronauts on a historic ride to the International Space Station.

When my kids were younger, we never missed our twice a year visits to Disneyland, in California and every other year to Disneyworld, in Florida.

Meet you at the entrance and race you to the Falcon, *"Smugglers Run..."*

Tigger

Landing

Is this real? Are they real? Are they coming? Are they already here? In this fast-moving world, these are fair questions. With the news reports and verification by some brilliant scientific minds of extraterrestrial visitation, it is time to discuss the possibility that we are not alone. On New Year's Eve, in 2018, on the hillside behind our home, we observed a most strange and mysterious object, hovering just above the ground. Its pulsating, interior light, held us spell bound for hours. Imagine the *Twilight Zone* theme music here.

We have become friends with our neighbors, Gene and Kelley, who live three doors away, on the same cul-de-sac. We who share this circular ending to a street, are fortunate enough to live on the very edge of civilization. Beyond our property lines, lies the wild and wonderful desert. As a true fan of *Close Encounters,* I look for locations, such as Devil's Tower Wyoming, as possible landing sites for crafts and creatures who are not of this world.

Ours is a landscape that has its own sights and sounds. On a moonlit night there are shapes and shadows in the desert, that not only resemble creatures from another world but seem to move and find voice on the desert wind. A few weeks ago, lounging on their back patio, enjoying a glass of wine, I noticed that their property, backing up into a deep canyon, would be a perfect landing site for such visitors. When I mentioned this, our neighbors fell silent and I noticed that they were ill-at-ease for a few moments.

I am certainly not suggesting that our newfound pals are extraterrestrial, but I will say that they did select a perfect residence, if they ever wanted to entertain guests from "out-of-town..."

Just Sayin'
Tigger

Corn Dogs

"It was Labor Day weekend, I was seventeen, I bought a Coke and some gasoline..." (Tim McGraw)

If I say, "County Fair," what is the first thing that comes to your mind; Food, rides, livestock, rodeo, the warm summer sun, a spectacular array of farm equipment or perhaps a pretty girl? For me, the answer is all of the above! My lifelong pretty prairie Kansas friend, Walt, claims it's "The Midway!"

I actually have to go into some serious training before we hop into the buggy, to head for the fair. I need exercise, diet, lots of water and whatever else it takes to be ready for a bit of porcine dining. For my surfing pals that means "piggin' out!"

I pity the vegetarian who goes to the county fair. What in the world could they eat? Just kidding. We have some wonderful vegan neighbors who have taught us so much about wise dining choices... I have just been a cowboy so long, that I'm still holding out for the carrot roping event in that rodeo arena.

Fact is I love artichokes, onion rings, baked potatoes, and mushrooms. I also have a fondness for pumpkin, rhubarb-strawberry, apple pie and that great American vegan standby, cotton candy.

I will never forget the first time my sidekick Wayne from Texas, looked up at our waitress and in his sweet Austin drawl asked, *"Do you have any fried cheese?"* Up until that moment I had never heard of such a thing, but they sure do have it at the fair.

Imagine my surprise when, enjoying a corn dog, I was told that it was not a vegetarian delicacy. It did however buoy my spirits, when I discovered that tequila is distilled from cactus and is therefore on the veggie menu.

I love the smell of the churro trailer on the afternoon breeze. What a day!

"And a heart don't forget somethin' like that..."

Tigger

The Time Machine

What ever happened to presentation skills? Immediately one thinks of speaking in public or rehearsing for a play, but I refer to the art of presenting a physical object to another human being, the sharing of a gift.

Recently, my friend John asked, rather mysteriously, when my actual birthday was, and I told him. We were preparing to perform the Righteous Brothers hit song, "Soul and Inspiration." He was coming over for some rehearsal time and a football game. John requested, rather straight forwardly, if he might have an uninterrupted thirty minutes of my attention during his visit. My response, being friends, was absolutely! What in the world could he have up his sleeve? An insurance pitch, a religious invitation or perhaps an investment idea… Who knew?

At the appointed time, I was invited into my own kitchen, where we sat face to face across the table. John is one fine storyteller and could hold a barrel full of monkeys spellbound, therefore I was prepared to listen and be enthralled. My friend produced a bubble wrapped parcel. *"Open it,"* he said with much enthusiasm and when I did, I found a wonderful surprise.

Inside the opaque wrapping was a beautiful Vostok watch. A model created and designed for precision time keeping under every condition. From outer space, to deep underwater exploration, this beauty is reliable and secure from anything mother earth and beyond might send to assault its beautiful crystal.

It's been a year now since this treasure was revealed to me. Each time I pause to look at my time-peace, to check on the progression of our comings and goings in the solar adventure, I am reminded how precious a gift from a friend truly is.

Now you know what I have up my sleeve. It's a handsome, accurate time piece, that will last my lifetime...

Thanks,
Tigger

Talk

My friend, Harry Nilsson, sang it softly and clearly, *"Everybody's talking'..."* This sweet ballad, composed by the great Fred Neil, was a masterpiece. The theme from the film, *Midnight Cowboy*, was an absolute mouthful of truth. *"Everybody's talking at me I don't hear a word their saying only the echoes of my mind..."* No wonder it was a Grammy Hall of Fame winner.

Talk: I hear it on the airplane, from the seat just behind me, in the elevator on my way up to a board meeting and in the conference room before, during and after the meeting. I hear it from folks on cell phones in the grocery store and at the checkout counter. Talk, talk, talk. How can it be, with so many words issuing forth, that so little communication is taking place? I wonder...

I have always loved language. My children and family love words and phrases and we often connect by sharing quotes from songs, films, plays and from our adventures. *"A mote of dust, suspended in a sunbeam..."*

Description of earth by Carl Sagan. *"We are but a moment's sunlight, fading in the grass..."* (Chet Powers, from the song, "Get Together"). *"Of course, you know, this means war..."* (Bugs Bunny). *"I'm more afraid of bein' nothing, than I am of being hurt!"* (Tom Cruz in Days of Thunder). *"I have a Dream..."* (Dr.

Martin Luther King). So much power in so few words.

Perhaps we simply talk too much and think too little. *"Smile though your heart is breaking..."* (Charlie Chaplin and John Turner). *"Follow your bliss..."* (Joseph Campbell).

Heading forward, a part of my New Year's resolution is to decrease the quantity and increase the quality, of my every spoken thought. I don't want to just talk; I want to truly speak. A family develops its energy, power, and respect, in the words they share and the thought and spirit they put into their discourse. *"People stopping staring I can't see their faces only the shadows of their eyes."*

Perhaps, *"We don't need no stinkin' badges after all!"*
Tigger

Calico Ghost Town

The desert night is cold and very dark. The breeze whispers across the moonless landscape. Firelight flickers out into the darkness and turns the Joshua trees into alien sentinels, watching. This is indeed a ghost town. Just now, my tent and sleeping bag look very warm and inviting but that is not my destination. I am a brand-new boy scout, and this is to be my night of initiation.

Standing, back to the fire, the two leaders place a blindfold carefully around my eyes and ears and in silence, lead me off into the wilderness. As we leave my fellow scouts behind to tend the fire, I hear their voices slowly trailing off into the distance.

On my stumbling way, I try my best to be attentive to the feel and the sounds of the ground beneath my feet and the smell of the foliage and landscape around me. We wander in and out for about an hour and at last, after turning me around a half-dozen times, the scout master commands, *"Remain here, blindfold on, while you count to one-hundred by fives. Then see if you can find your way back to our camp."*

Lost! I have known scouts and leaders who were absolutely panicked by the mere thought of this moment. Alone in the dark forest with just a flashlight and my wits. The fact is, I was inspired and enthused by the opportunity to find my way.

"90...95...100..." Blindfold off, I allow my eyes to adjust to the night that surrounds me, and I strike out for camp. In a brief twenty minutes I am warming myself by the campfire when the leaders return. Astounded (and very disappointed) they stammer, *"How did you get here so fast?"* My response... *"I looked at the stars before you blindfolded me, and my return was easy."*

Whenever we are lost or confused, look up at the night sky. Your way and your purpose will come clear and be re-affirmed!

"Be Prepared..."
Tigger

The City

Is it strange that I can find great joy in something I miss so dearly? It's a cold and windy night in North Beach. Sandwiched between Telegraph and Russian Hill, the air is filled with the fragrance of Italian cooking, incoming fog, and the historic bay itself. I do love and miss my frequent visits to the city by the bay. I am standing across the blustery street from Vanessi's Restaurant, in company with my friend and Atlantic Records promotion master, Rich Totoian. We are huddled, laughing against the wind with Eric Clapton and Ginger Baker. The only one missing is Jack Bruce and we are told he will be along any moment. This is truly the cream of the crop and I am honored to be here with Rich, promoting *Disraeli Gears,* the album that will become the best-selling LP of all time, for this incredible group of rockers.

Cold and damp, we finally decide to head across and take up our reservations at the fabulous Vanessi's Restaurant. We are known here and if we were not, the great Eric Clapton would command the attention of any maître D. Once seated, the California Chardonnay and incredible San Francisco sourdough bread and butter arrive, as a preview to their famous escargot. At last, we see in the doorway, Jack Bruce and Sharon Nelson. Our party is complete. The steaks are on their way.

As I often do, when supper is finished in the city by the bay, I leave the warmth of a fine restaurant and head for Wolfback Ridge, to gaze out across the city lights and the great Pacific. Surrounded by the sweet fragrance of these hills, I utterly understand Tony Bennett and Otis Redding, as they express their heart's connection to San Francisco.

Me too...
Tigger

Hollister

From the Santa Barbara Harbor, we rode up the coastline in our little boat, to Gaviota. It's about 30 miles of beautiful, bumpy ride. To starboard, lay the sun drenched foothills of the historic Santa Ynez mountains, covered in orange, lemon and avocado trees. We were able to glimpse between the ancient rich green oaks in the fields to see deer, horses and watch with envy, red tail hawks, in pursuit of their lunch. We were also passing Rancho Del Cielo, The Ranch in the sky, the vacation home of President Ronald Reagan.

We were on our way to surf one of the most wonderful, carefully guarded shore breaks in the world. The only way to get to Hollister Ranch is by boat. We tied up carefully to a sturdy kelp fan, against the wind and waves, threw our boards over and swam and surfed with the seals, until our lips were blue, and our fingers looked like prunes.

There is something incredibly special about visiting places where most folks, including hard core surfers rarely go. Seated on our boards awaiting the next rich green rising wave, we can look down beneath us into the underwater sanctuary of the seals. Amidst the sun splashed kelp fans, we see some of the one hundred species of fish that live in these clear, coastal waters. This is home to Kelp bass, cabezon, sheepshead, horned shark, and senorita fish.

A sight that holds us spellbound, is the beautiful bright orange garibaldi perch, swimming gracefully amidst the forest of golden kelp, until we turn toward the beach and without a word takeoff on another smooth powerful wave.

Have you ever seen a Hollister surf logo on a shirt? Have you wondered if the wearer has ridden the rich blue-green shore break? They haven't! The closest most folks come, is driving through the inland town of Hollister, the seismic capital of California. I have often wondered why anyone would wear a shirt or jacket from a place they have never been.

Let's head up there together and share the real adventure.

We Ride Together,
Tigger

Valley Forge

Forge (definition): "To make or shape a metal object by heating it in a fire or furnace and beating or hammering it into the desired shape. To create a relationship or a new condition."

In my case the word means to forge, or shape a memory as strong as steel and as tender as my love for our Nation's birth.

On the road between Philadelphia and Lancaster, PA, I watched with great anticipation. As the trees and shrubs began to shroud the highway, I wished I had arrived during the daylight hours. The winter sun was well into its decent, when I pulled into the nearly empty parking lot and stepped out into frigid evening air. Having visited Valley Forge with my family on many a summer's day, this was a place I had dreamed of experiencing at night and in winter. Here I was.

As I passed through the park entrance, the snow began to fall in earnest and a cold breath of wind took me full in the face. The first chance I got, I left the trail and headed into the woods. Once beyond the sound of humanity, I simply stopped quite still and listened. It took a few mind-clearing moments but then, slowly and faintly, I could hear what I came for, the crackle of a campfire and the distant sound of hushed men's voices. The longer I paused and the harder I strained; I could hear the soft whinnying of hungry horses. I knew it. This was a place so rich with courage and history, that I was sure the spirits of those who fought here so bravely could not possibly have left.

The famous painting of our first president, kneeling in prayer beside his dapple-gray horse, Blueskin, brings a chill each time I stand before it. May we, each in our own way, find honor in this General, who so courageously led his rag-tag band of cold, hungry Americans. May we be the ones who bring our great nation back together!

Tigger

Wabi Sabi

There is nothing quite as wonderful as learning from our children. I am a richer man for realizing that my offspring have seen and done things I have never experienced and my respect for and attention to their stories and lessons, are for me, a living treasure.

"My Aunt Lynn died today, Dad." Simple words in text on the face of my iPhone. My son, to the west, California Chris and I have faced this moment often in our lives together. To the east, my son, Colorado Chris and I are working on a book together. He, the artist and I the author, spend many hours in conversation, meditation and creative connection.

In one of our recent communique's, he asked me about these two words, "wabi sabi." Although I have a deep and abiding respect for Japan and its rich culture, I had to admit that I did not know wabi sabi. Our Japanese friend, Kazu, inspired my understanding. Thus nothing lasts, nothing is perfect. The weathered wood of Kyoto's temples, the faces of the elderly and the wing of a time worn butterfly, all bear witness to the fact that nothing lasts, nothing is perfect or permanent. Both life and art are beautiful, not because they are perfect and eternal but because they are imperfect and fleeting.

All of us live through both gain and loss. Having lost a child and a grandchild, we know the deep sense of mourning that attends such an event. We do not however, forget the feeling of joy and elation, at the arrival of a new life into our world.

Those of you who know me well and long, are aware of my positive approach to life and its challenges. Those of you who know me best, are aware that I am touched very deeply by love and loss. Melancholy is not a stranger to my soul. Bless the rough edges, the sunshine and shadows; the wabi sabi.

Tigger

Treasure

It was a cold, sunny day on the Little Susitna River. The zodiac boat was screaming into the wind and up-river into no-man's land. As Nanook (Rick) and I bounced along together, we simply enjoyed the bumps, the weather and the incredible wild beauty that is Alaska.

My friend and spirit brother of over a-half-century had agreed to go treasure hunting to try and find a spot where no white man had ever set foot before. We left Hooligan's Island and after two hours of windblown wonder, we nodded one to the other and turned out of the fast rushing current. We pulled the sleek grey rubber boat up onto the sandy beach of a deserted island. We were there! To tell the truth, the ride had bounced our morning coffee out of us, and we needed to stop to relieve that situation.

As we ventured on to the sandspit of our treasure island, we were dive bombed by a pair of nesting Aleutian terns. Somewhere in the grass patches and river rocks, there must have been a nest and we were being warned to steer clear! When we finally sat down to our jacket molded sandwiches, I asked Rick, *"Did you see it?"* He simply answered *"Yes."* And so we set her free, climbed aboard and headed back down river to confirm our sighting.

We were about halfway back to camp when we both spotted the

target. There, on the bank of the *little Su,* was a beautiful moose antler, either shed or knocked off in last season's mating battles. To me it was a most welcome bit of art and certainly a treasure for the ages. When you come to visit us, two-thousand miles away, in southern Nevada, I will challenge you to spot the sun-bleached moose antler on the Jeremiah Johnson memorial here in our monastery.

Tigger

Where You Been?

Gathered, family style, for breakfast in a midwestern diner, we were on a long road trip. *"Hungry,"* was the word of the morning. I loved bringing the family along, so we could be together during those special young years in the lives of our children. We were often three or four in company and that group included one of our kid's friends. I had discovered, if you play it right, every moment can be an adventure. We were certainly living one on this trip.

In that mom and pop café, the food being served around us smelled scrumptious. The little room was packed and it appeared that it was going to be awhile before our bacon, eggs and pancakes would arrive, so my wife suggested that we play a game. You may not believe it but I love interactive fun stuff with the troops.

To our good fortune, the place mats in front of us were imprinted with a map of the United States and this offered the opportunity to share some memories. The first game/question was: *"Where is your favorite place on this map and why?"* The answers came fast and furious. *"Phoenix,"* and the reason, *"the pool at the Desert Rose Motel where we swam and played long into the desert night."* The bottom of the pool was so old and rough and the chlorine so heavy, that we all had holes in our soles before we climbed into bed.

The next favorite was Hawaii and the bright-eyed reason was, *"The coconut pancakes on the terrace with Portuguese sausage and coconut syrup."* One by one we began to learn that our kids had truly loved our adventures and appreciated having been included. From Valley Forge to Yellowstone, from Yosemite to Disneyworld, from San Diego to Boston, we had done a great job of including our offspring in our experiences.

As the interest in the game tapered off, our son's pal asked, why we all don't mark on the map the states we have been through. My wife looked at me and exclaimed *"That's no fun... You've been to all of them!"* I just had to smile. I have spoken in every major city in America and nearly all of the secondary ones too. I love every moment of the places, the faces and spaces that we have shared.

Tigger

Educare (Ed-you-car-eh)

I was honored by the invitation to share. The program was titled, "How to win teachers and influence kids!" Having been a poor student myself, I guessed that I was either the very best or the very worst choice for a speaker. On my entry backstage, I assumed that there would be at least 20 attendees. I was on a panel of guests which included, Monty Hall, TV host, Gralin Landon, publicist for Elvis Presley, our host and moderator Lady Ethel Booth, and Little Dougie Cox, Program Director from radio station KRLA.

The audience was made up of audio-visual educators from across the nation. Imagine my surprise when the curtains opened and the Melodyland theater was SRO. Yipes! One by one, Ms. Booth introduced us to the audience. I listened intently to each presenter, trying to prepare myself for the opportunity to come. As the speakers, one by one, told us how wonderful and famous they were, I thought about how I might address the subject that had been given us. Once introduced, I surveyed the sullen faces of the educators and then dove in.

"What," I asked, *"is the meaning of the word educare?"* The response was a silent stare! Teachers, I discovered do not like being tested! Finally, one gentleman in the front row, in a rather disgusted voice, replied, *"That is a stupid question, it is of course the verb to teach!"* I let the moment sink in and finally replied with the sound of a game show buzzer when a contestant has given a wrong answer, *"Buzzzzz... Wrong,"* I replied, *"Educare means to lead out and that is why your students do not respond enthusiastically to your teaching! We never teach,"* I added, *"we only awaken the natural curiosity in others."*

It took a few moments but finally the educators before me, began to applaud and the rest of the event was a big hit. This once resistant audience became wonderful friends and clients who booked and took me all over America to share the enthusiasm of *"Educare."*

Tigger

Baseline

In 1852, in a little Mormon settlement in Southern California, Henry Washington, a government surveyor, placed a marker on the hill overlooking the fort. That monument was to be the starting point for all the surveying done from that day to this, in San Bernardino, CA. It is now Baseline Street.

I love the term, starting point. It indicates beginnings and encourages measurements. When I celebrate my annual physical exam, my Doctor and I set out a baseline for blood pressure, oxygen uptake and weight. That way we have a starting point from which to observe and manage my health and wellbeing.

As the lead off batter on a baseball team, Coach Clarkson would look down the baseline to see where the third baseman is playing. If he was off the bag he would say, *"Cox drop that bunt right down the baseline."* Whether we are navigating in the open ocean, climbing into the King's Canyon Wilderness or trying to decide if a tennis serve or line drive is in or out, we use a baseline as our guide.

When the year turns from an old one to a new one, I look at my baseline and turn my eyes toward becoming a better me, physically, financially, emotionally and spiritually.

This way, when I get to first base, you can drive me into home. Happy, healthy prosperous New Year to us one and all!

Tigger

Big Box Day

In the muted first light of dawn, the old battered pickup truck comes slowly up our street. It is a sight that I have seen before. The couple inside are hunting. Searching among the trash of others, for what just might be a treasure to them. It's big box day in our neighborhood.

For those of us who have eyes and hearts, this bi-monthly happening is truly an opera of grand proportions. In front of each home, beside the two trash containers, one for garbage and one for recycling, you can see boxes and bags loaded with stuff that wouldn't fit in the containers. From yard trimmings to hardware of all kinds, the Grinch would be salivating. I see misfit toys, exercise equipment, bedding, yard tools, furniture and anything and everything else our throwaway society has decided we no longer need or want.

Today I saw something new... I saw, leaning against the trash container of our elderly neighbors, the aluminum bars of a small dog gate. The kind installed to keep little critters out of mischief in a home. Most people wouldn't even notice or recognize this item placed in the trash but I did. It is the sign of the passing of a very special dearly loved companion.

Often, on my walkabout and climb up Doug's mountain, I would pass this home and stop to visit with the sweet old man that lives there. He would be out, very slowly walking his ancient yorkie terrier. Each time we stopped to chat, this wonderful little furry friend would head in my direction for some love and each time he would move a bit more slowly. My heart breaks for that couple and I feel a kinship with them.

I hope that the couple in the old battered pickup found some treasures on their hunt today.

Tigger

Change

Suddenly the temperature has dropped. Not creepy-crawly dropped but down twenty degrees overnight. What once was a breeze, is now a brisk wind and it brings the fragrance of pine, juniper, and oak with it. A whole mountainside of leaves have danced their last and there is a sprinkling of powdered sugar on the mountain tops. Praise be, the season has changed.

This year as the desert wind brings autumn to our valley, it also brings one of the joys of life on the edge of the city and that is, new faces. Across the street, a moving van has arrived and what was an empty house, is becoming a home again. The license plate on the vehicle out front is from another state. Fresh faces begin to come and go.

We are a self-appointed welcoming committee and there is nothing quite like the first handshake from a new neighbor. We cannot tell what tomorrow will bring but the first moments set the tone for a bright and peaceful future. We have welcomed many newcomers to our "hood" and they have proven to be of every mindset. From besties for life, to absolute reclusive folks, with the ultimate of respect, we have welcomed them all.

Our newest arrivals are a treasure chest of stories to tell and memories to share. What are the chances? The young lady revealed to us, that her father worked for a company in the Midwest, for whom I performed so often. I considered her dad a dear friend. Her husband and his family were railroaders and there is nothing that Sharon and I enjoy more, than riding the rails. (On the inside of the train of course.)

This is a change that brightens our world and adds to the joy of our holidays. Our neighbors, The Kelly's, have become fast friends and we could not be more honored.

This holiday season, give yourself a wonderful gift and say howdy to your neighbors. Particularly the newest arrivals.

Welcome,
from Tigger

Le Rêve

"Le Rêve," the dream, in French, reminds me that I have lived on and in that castle for much of my life. I am indeed a dreamer but as my wonderful friend Bob Buerger once said, *"Doug may be a dreamer, but he is also one who fights and perseveres until he makes his dream a reality."* Tis' true. For years I have kept my "dream sheet" in my pocket, on my nightstand, in my car and on the lectern before me, when doing a presentation.

Recently I had the gift of speaking to a group of students at a magnificent school in West Jordan, Utah. During my prayers and preparation to meet these young wizards we have named millennials, I wondered how I might make my dream sheet idea more relevant to them. Then it hit me! Where is it that these bright, intuitive young people focus their every waking moment and the answer is...on their smart phones!

During the class, as I always do with my audiences, I had them write on a 3X5 card before them, their dreams and their hearts desire, only this time I invited them to write their dreams vertically on the blank paper. I then had them shoot a photo of their own signed aphorism, edit, and save it as wallpaper on their phone screen.

What is your dream or as Dorothy, in The Wizard of Oz put it,

"My heart's desire?" As days and time swirl around us, we have a tendency to let our dreams slip out of our reality and into the realm of fantasy. Nothing could be more dangerous. Dreams are the script for the movie of your life. Every moment of your life from your first cry at birth, to your last breath on earth, you will be on your way. For most of us, we will be, sadly, on somebody else's way, living out the dreams and commands of others. Take command today and give yourself the gift of the dream, Le Reve...

Now, each time you look down at your device, instead of seeing what someone else thinks is important, you will be looking at and reinforcing your own precious, dreams!

My Dream Is!...
Tigger

Meadowlark

Outside the farmhouse window, a sound drifts in from the fragrant meadow. It is a sweet, liquid warbling song, new to my ear. As a curious young lad of five, I wanted not only to hear more of this concert but to see who was making this joyful noise! Without a word, I placed my breakfast dishes on the sink and pushed my way out through the squeaky kitchen screen door.

With much anticipation, I stepped into the warm southern California morning sunlight.

The lilting sound was not hard to follow. It led me to the wood-rail fence that separated our human world, from that of the green pasture and the animals grazing therein. Climbing up to lean on the topmost rail, I looked out into the meadow to see this small brightly colored soloist, perched on the top of a sunflower shrub. I leaned there, entranced for what seemed like forever, when I felt a hand touch my arm. *"Do you like that sound Dougbert?"* It was my mother, who had followed me out of the house and into my adventure. I responded that I thought the song was quite beautiful and wondered at the name of the little bird who was making such a big and beautiful sound. *"That is a meadowlark,"* she replied. Then she added, *"Would you like to be able to whistle her tune?"* Of course, I was excited and ready to learn.

It took a few lessons but within the week I was talking to the meadowlarks in and around our land. I enjoyed every minute of my communication with the beautiful, ubiquitous yellow and black wonders of our southern California farm.

I learned a great lesson in appreciation, when at age forty I was stricken with Bell's palsy and due to the paralysis in my facial muscles, lost my ability to whistle. Do a Google search for Western Meadowlark sounds and share the glory with me...

Tigger

Whaleshead

The little twin-engine jet slipped down through the cloud deck and burst out into the clear. Off the port wing a lighthouse appeared nestled on the coastline and below me I saw a beautiful harbor. Touching down in Crescent City, California is a beautiful experience.

Visiting my daughter and her man, made it even more wonderful. I have driven through on highway 101 many times but this was my first real get off my horse and hang my hat, for a night's stopover. At their suggestion, we headed out to Whaleshead Beach for a hike and an adventure.

Most mornings, as my readers know, I am heading up the dry and dusty trail, to the summit of my desert mountain. This was a complete and joyful change of venue. Down the wooded trail, along the fresh running stream, was my entry into paradise. As a light rain fell on our heads and filled up the ruts on the path, I took great joy in dancing between the raindrops and accidentally on purpose, stepping in the puddles. I am a puddle jumper you know!

At trails end is a beautiful curve of dark, rich sand, decorated with shells, driftwood, and the most beautiful rocks I have ever seen, from the smallest to the largest, which is Whaleshead Rock. When the waves hit this huge sea stack, it casts off water like a whale in full blow. I saw mushrooms, wild roses, wild strawberries, and huckleberry bushes. Oh MY!

When you come to the close of a perfect day, it simply must end in a wonderful Mexican restaurant. There we were, embraced by the fragrance of Mexican delights, margaritas y cervezas in hand, and a serving of Poncho's scrumptious comida, Mexicana, on a piping hot plate. I am one very blessed dad!

Brookings Harbor is a place to stop and breathe-in the wonders of nature and the love of family...

Happy Tigger

Next time... Indian Sands Trail and Gold Beach!

Harvest Moon

The little girl walks slowly down the dusty lane. Against the darkness, she clings tightly to the old man's hand. The evening seems caught between the warmth of an Indian summer day and the coolness of the fall night, waiting just around the corner. He has passed eighty-four summers on this land; this is only her third. As with all of his children and all of his grandchildren, they are headed to the end of the lane to fulfill an annual tradition. It is important to have traditions and memories. It is also important to have something to believe in.

In the distance, a whippoorwill calls goodbye to summer and on either side of the road the cornstalks rustle gently in the faint breeze. Change is in the air. At the end of the lane by the old fence, he lifts the child to his shoulders and turns to face the east. Something very special is about to happen.

The little girl watches in awe, as the great golden ball climbs above the rim of the earth. Cast loose from its moorings, the giant orb rises into the starlit sky.

"My child," says the old man softly, *"a harvest moon is the sign that all that we have worked for, will come to pass. It is the promise that the earth will send forth rewards to match our labors and our prayers."*

The old man stayed long that night at the fence by the end of the lane. Life, like the adventure, does not go on forever. Then at last, tradition fulfilled and memories in heart, he and his sleepy passenger turn slowly and head back down the dusty roadway, back through the cornfield, toward the light in the little farmhouse window and something to believe in.

Tonight... Look up at the wonder and share!

Tigger

Wham!

With red light and siren announcing its arrival, the shiny firetruck roared down the rainy Santa Barbara street and turned into the wet parking lot. The two unusual passengers, Santa and his Elf, dropped to the ground and headed up the stairs into the old building. With loaded pack, the annual Christmas visit to the special children's home had begun.

Every year, in Goleta, CA. the Breakfast Optimist Club, sends members out to share simple gifts with children who would receive none. That year it was my blessing to be an Elf in service. Once in the classroom, the faces before us brightened with anticipation.
As we took our seats, the young treasures came pushing and shoving, to get closer to the jolly old soul in the red suit. From hiding in shyness to shrieking out loud, they gathered before us. One by one they took their place on Santa's lap, shared their secret wishes and received their candy canes and gifts.

Finally, the last shy young lad who had held back from the visit, found his way forward and gingerly climbed up on the lap of the stranger in familiar garb.

No matter how Santa reached out, the boy spoke not a word. Finally, my friend asked, *"What have you been thinking about?"* After a long silent space, the little man held up his hand like an imaginary cowboy pistol... *"Wham!"* he shouted... The room fell silent. The nurse who had accompanied the boy, dropped down to one knee and started to cry. This incredibly special child had never spoken until that moment he connected with a stranger from a service club! This was Christmas treasure, enough for a lifetime.

Tigger Claus

Lost!

The co-en flannel blanket where she slept every night, was empty. She loved that cozy place and was always there in the morning. Where could she have gone. We turned on ABC News to see if they could help us find her but their young newscaster only pointed toward the mou-ans and suggested that she may have bi-en off more than she could chew, by heading into the desert all alone. We did not understand. The police officer sounded so sympathetic when he exclaimed, *"So... you've lost your ki-en, eh?"* It was like we had fallen asleep in one familiar world and awakened in another. The Twilight Zone! What in the world were they all talking about?

Animal Rescue... perhaps they could help us. *"Let me get this straight,"* queried the animal control officer, *"Your ki-en was not on her co-en blanket in the morning and you think that she may have run off to the mou-ans, right?"*

"Perhaps she was simply sm-en with an attractive mou-an lion..." I had no idea what was going on, but I read in the paper that a park ranger had frozen her hands, because it was way below zero and she could not find her mi-ens...

It seems that our ki"tt"en climbed off of her co"tt"on blanket, walked away or was lured away by a handsome moun"t"ain lion and a faithful park ranger, without her mi"tt"ens got frostbite trying to find her.

Like a frame without a photo, the loss of proper spelling, pronunciation and use of our blessed language, will put us in grave danger of losing our wonderful way. Most impor-antly, without our "t's" we would never find our beloved ki"tt"en!

Tigger is very thankful that we have not yet lost our "GG's!"

Magic Leaves

Santa Barbara was our home. It is a place of azure skies, blue sparkling water and sunlight, that sweeps daily across the horizon from east to west, bathing the foothills with the gift of life. One of the beneficiaries of that life- giving-light, is the California Bay tree. A hardwood, standing strong and tall beside the pacific oak, madrone, black oak and sycamore, it is a glorious, proud green giant.

Its fragrant leaves are often found dried and added to slow cook recipes, such as spaghetti, roast potatoes, lentil soup and a thousand other dishes. They have an even more romantic and historic place in the hearts and noses of our family.

As we arrived, one by one, to take up residence in this beautiful, historic community, I guided my family members to the top of Coyote Road and assembled them beneath the branches of a hundred-year-old bay tree. I explained that it was a "magic" tree and proceeded to present them with a leaf from this glorious hardwood. As we each crinkled the treasures in our hands and held them up to our noses, we knew for sure that this was a magic moment, in a special time.

Today, scattered to the four-winds as we are, I sent off a note to each of those loved ones, enclosing in the snail-mail envelope, a fresh magic leaf from the foothills of Santa Barbara. On arrival we will all, once again, crinkle the green treasure in our hands and hearts.

You may, if you wish, join us. In your spice cabinet there is a bottle or tin of bay leaves. Open it carefully, breath in the captured aroma of the Santa Barbara foothills and hold the precious leaf in your hands. And once again we are there… Together!

Tigger

Darkness

Perhaps you have heard of our Famous Las Vegas Buffets? Inexpensive food, all you can eat and depending on where you go, yummy! In just such a setting, we were sharing an evening of dining and storytelling with two of our besties, when I noticed a family sitting at the table just across from us. From my vantage point I saw what appeared to be grandparents, a young couple and two children: she about five and he about two years of age.

The small boy, in his highchair, sat turned directly in toward me, facing his family. As his mom went off to gather another plate of food, I noticed that he was blind. On her departure from the table, I observed his reaction to her exit and I saw in him that heightened awareness that unsighted people often develop. His little hands reached up as if to say, *"Don't leave me here!"* She paid no mind. On her return, plate in hand, he recognized her arrival and reached out, again expressing his gratefulness for her presence. In both cases, the woman neither touched him, acknowledged his presence or spoke to him.

Throughout the whole evening, although the other members of the family interacted quite normally, no one ever made an overture to this little man. It seemed to me as if his darkness was far greater than just the absence of sight. Children only know and become what we share with them. We are the gardeners of their becoming!

All I could think about was the common expression, *"Out of sight, out of mind..."*

I felt a loneliness, Tigger

PS: What an experience it is to be working diligently on a book, page after page, only to discover that the world into which the book will be published is a whole new one. At this re-write, every buffet in the city of Las Vegas is closed and may never open the same again. This does not change the experience, captured by your author in the days past. It simply offers the opportunity to become our new and better selves on awakening.

The Ride

I have always loved horses and mules. If there ever was a time in my life where I knew that I hadn't lost my senses but indeed had come to them, it would be my days around these wonderful beasts of burden. Those of you who have never shared the companionship of a pack animal, will have to ride along with us in your imagination.

It is a dark and wonderful night along the Walker River, in the heart of the Sierra Nevada mountains. Beneath a billion stars and warm in my sleeping bag, I am resting up for tomorrow's ride up into the lake country. My son, Dave, safe in his own bag, reminds me that we are not allowed to go to sleep until we have spotted at least two satellites passing overhead. That accomplished, I am an excellent sleeper, so the roar of the river, full on in its raging glory, puts me into joyful repose and the morning arrives fast, bright and wonderful.

At the pack station we are assigned our vehicles for the days to come and I begin by inspecting and saying howdy to my mount. Whether it is on a ranch, out on the range or up in the mountains, there is something wonderful about these critters and companions. They have a unique and comforting smell. Their size and sheer muscle mass are a wonder beneath us. Steady, whether on a country road or up the side of a rock-strewn mountainside, they are surefooted and responsible. On this ride, crossing the creek, I was reminded of the validity of the old adage, *"You can lead a horse to water, but you can't make him drink..."* Tis true!

During our nights on the mountain, the nickering sound of our equine limousine's at tether was a comforting sound.

Tigger

Shadows

Why is it that the photographs of Ansel Adams, hold so many of us spell bound? The great photographer and naturalist would answer, *"Shadow, that magic darkness that shades and shifts the light, bringing out the secrets of our mental artwork."*

Sunshine and Shadows: The World of Ansel Adams is the book that tells the story of the great artist's undying love affair with the contrasting colors that give us chiaroscuro, light falling unevenly from a particular direction.

On my mountain, where I love to climb each day, I am surrounded and entranced by the fact that the desert sun, spills its magical light onto sparse southwestern life. It clings to the canvas of a landscape, that lives and hangs on, in the searing heat and the absence of water.

I am a photographer. Definitely an amateur but I am extremely proud of my craft. I have the good fortune of knowing some exceptional photographers that produce some exquisite images and I am honored by their coaching. One of them, a sports photographer of high esteem, once paid me what I considered, a terrific compliment. We were discussing an upgrade in camera equipment and he said, *"Forget about a new camera. You have a fantastic eye."* He helped me understand that my photography has given me a new set of eyes that see what others do not and allow me to capture moments and images, others would pass by. The first and last thing I see when I am hunting images is the sunlight and shadows that fall on the object.

Shadows have come into my life in so many forms and figures: Nanook's totem brother, Tim, named his Alaskan dog, Shadow. The master programmer, actor and great dee-jay, Shadoe Stevens, simply chose a different spelling for his professional name. The Academy Award winning love song from the film, *The Sandpiper* is, "The Shadow of Your Smile." How many have I forgotten? While you are "standing in the shadow of love," help?

For me it is the shadows of those things, that touch our lives, that frame our light and bring joyful vision to our living.

Tigger

Different

They were the best that ever was... Stan Kenton, June Christie and the Four Freshman! Some of the greatest musicians, vocalists and performers in the world, all on one stage. I had flown to see them in San Francisco and loved it so much, I drove to Los Angeles to live it all again.

What? You don't know who those people were? This was the best music ever created and performed, except for one thing...You have groups and music that you believe to be the very best. That is the joy of art. It is always growing and changing, drawing in new minds, ages and hearts and that is, as it should be.

Think about it now. Do you have a favorite artist, song or group? Me too. Now the $64,000 question: Is my music better than yours or is yours superior to mine? You know the answer. It's about time, space, memories, moments and life. When I hear people of my generation exclaim that today's music is awful, stupid or just plain terrible, I understand. I don't agree but I hope that it will always be so, that my music was the best that ever was.

In every generation music is always a part of playing back to us, what we are thinking and feeling, helping us to get through our time. If the music of our greatest generation hadn't carried us successfully through some very tough times, you wouldn't be listening to your music right now.

Do yourself a favor! Do a Google search for Reminiscing by The Little River Band, and give it a listen. Add in the names of your favorite performers and save me a dance. I may not love your music but I sure as hell love you!

Tigger

Song Dog

The opera began, the moment the sun slipped below the horizon. It sounded like the whole family was celebrating, yaps from the alpha and his lady and yips from the little ones. It was a joyful ruckus!

I realize that I have written about coyotes before, but these mystical canines deserve more than a casual mention. With the construction that goes on around our quiet, desert haven, we haven't heard or seen these friends quite as often and I miss them. John Denver sang, *"Why they try to tear the mountains down to bring in a couple more, more people, more scars upon the land!"* The people that were here for thousands of years before we invaded, called them "song dogs." Makes good sense, as they can howl down the sun and sing up the moon. Coyotes are known by native peoples as tricksters. It is amazing but true. I cannot count the times I have turned to point out one of these tawny beauties to my kids, only to look back and find that they have disappeared.

One Sierra Nevada summer evening, we sat spellbound around the campfire, listening to a Navajo Medicine Woman tell us the story of how coyote tricked the doves. *"The trickster sat at the bottom of the tree,"* she said *"and threatened the family of doves. If you don't send one dove down to me, I will come up and eat them all."*

Coyote is an irresponsible and trouble-making character. Often the best example of how not to act, he is also one of the most important and revered characters in Navajo mythology. He is admired for his careless energy and his suggestion that all things are possible. In the Native way, things, like people, are not all good or bad but a bit of both, with the opportunity to become better as we learn and grow. The coyote stories about lizard, buffalo and giant, are all wonderful teaching tools for growth and understanding.

Coyote was wise to use all the emotions of the situation to feed his hungry family. Hearing the coyote's threat, the mother dove thought, *"I would be better off losing one and keeping the others,"* so she sent one of her young down to the coyote. That was easy, thought the coyote and so he did the same thing over and over until all the young doves were gone. When the mother, finally realized that she had been tricked, she flew off singing her mourning song... *"Juhwaypoo-Juhwaypoo!"*

Coyote also brings the joy of discovery as our young friend, eighteen-year-old *Alex*, revealed when she said, *"Something is moving out there in the darkness."* It was a song dog who came to join our evening on the patio.

Tigger

Four Jacks

It is a warm spring afternoon in our desert. The breeze is blowing from the north across my face and the fragrance is a tease of summer on its way. From my seat on our patio, I am putting blue pen notes on a yellow pad. A new chapter is being born. Happy time.

It's a true half-mile to the top of my mountain, with a deep canyon to the right. From that canyon something is moving, and it is heading my way, at a surprisingly good clip. By the time I figure out that what I am seeing is more than one, I realize the only things out and about on our monastery who move in a group, are coyotes and quail. Flashing through the creosote and sage, the color seems right but coyotes in the afternoon would be highly unlikely.

One of the great joys of our southwest, is that we are forever surprised by what happens next. I watched and waited, not daring to turn away, as coyotes are known to disappear in the blink of an eye. My focus was rewarded by the sight of a group of four jack rabbits, heading hell-bent-for-leather across my view. I have learned in the desert, to watch now and blink later, because this is a world of come and go, so fast. They might as well have been young kangaroos, as they were bounding at about four to five feet a hop. At least three feet tall from tail to ears, they were a wonderful, humorous sight.

We are so used to seeing cotton tails with their truly powderpuff cabooses, that these critters with their black tails, were quite a sight. It was Mark Twain, having seen their huge ears, who wrote in his book, *Roughing It,* that they "looked like Jackass Rabbits." Jacks are rightly black tail hares who can grow to be a hearty ten pounds apiece. They are active mostly at night, except ours, who come frequently all day long for water, while the young'uns remain in the form, their scraped-out home, with their long ears flattened against their backs.

These super-bunnies are breakfast for many predators. Coyotes, bobcats, horned owls, and the babies, are snake bait for sure. If you startle these rascals, they can run at such speed that coyotes often just let them be. I have been photographing these athletic creatures since the day they arrived and am fascinated by the fact that they always arrive, down the canyon and up to the north, returning toward the south and back up into their mysterious residence.

Four Jacks...Not a bad hand...
Tigger

Sweet Freedom

Dr. Who, the director, steps onto the stage and speaks into a crackling microphone. *"Today students, we have a special guest speaker. He has come to us as a friend of Officer Tony Careccia and the Coconut Creek Seminole Casino."* The students waste no time in rolling their eyes and sinking down in their seats... Another boring assembly! *"With a career in the music business, radio and The Hard Rock, please welcome Doug Cox!"*

Michael McDonald's voice fills the auditorium, *"Shine Sweet Freedom, shine your light on me!"* I run up onto the stage, hug the Director and turn to a sea of doubting young faces. *"I enjoyed hearing your comments in the hallway just now. Oh yes... I was listening... Who's the geezer over there?* (Much giggling and embarrassing looks.) *Now you know... The Geez is your speaker."*

That's how it begins, and it always ends with a fantastic group of young Americans standing, holding their *"Dream Sheets"* in the air and cheering for themselves. I have never met a person of any age, who does not have a dream, a wish, a hope. It is my pleasure, that throughout the world, I have had the blessing of reminding folks of this marvelous truth. My greatest joy is doing so in concert, with bright, young people. To see their faces change, when they hear about the loss of our daughter in a traffic accident and how as a young boy I too was molested. To feel them, whatever their circumstances, rise-up in understanding of the power and possibilities for themselves, is a moment that turns every day into Christmas for this Cowboy/Geezer.

At the conclusion of my presentations, I always stay to greet and connect with any student or students that may wish to share a howdy. In nearly every group, there is at least one who stands back, until the auditorium clears and then approaches, to say in a shy and quiet voice, *"May I ask you something?"* The question, like the conversation, is always about a family challenge. The content is too personal to reveal here but the level of abuse and violence that is visited on innocent, young people is astounding. Tears just now as I write.

See you in the all-purpose room...
Tigger

White Bird

Whenever the song came on the radio, I stopped what I was doing and turned it up. *"White Bird, in a golden cage, on a winter's day, in the rain..."* The group performing was "It's a Beautiful Day," and I loved David LaFlamme's classically trained electric violin and the vocal by Pattie Santos. This was a symphony of the heart, in the days of the Grateful Dead, Jefferson Airplane and Carlos Santana. A song from the summer of love.

Imagine my surprise, today, when we were visited by just such a White Bird. The messenger, from 1967, flew in on the desert wind to land gracefully on the hillside behind our home. A traditional water-bird in the arid southwestern desert, oh my! It was an egret with feathers so perfectly white that they lighted up the afternoon landscape of the monastery. This was not my first surprise, that came on the wings of a "White Bird."

One weekend in my Santa Barbara home, I drove to the beach for some body surfing, in the cool fresh salt water of the springtime pacific. A little chilled and with sand in my teeth, I climbed into my old caddy to warm up. Hoping to catch a weak signal from my L.A. radio station, I punched the pre-set for 1110, KRLA and there it was, static but wonderful. "White Bird..." How could that be... Our station was trying to play more songs, so a record of nearly six minutes was not supposed to be on the air.

As is so often the case, the employee knows far better than the employer and my friend and DJ, Gary Marshall, was enlightening Southern California with an unapproved taste of a far more "Beautiful Day!" Gary and I still laugh about that experience and his good taste in music. *"White Bird, she must fly..."*

Tigger

Tween

When I was seven years of age, I had my tonsils removed. In those days this was a common procedure. After my release from the hospital, our eye, ear, nose and throat doc told us to be extremely careful about overdoing it during the next five-ten days. I remember three things about that surgical adventure so very long ago. The first was the smell of ether on the little juice strainer they placed over my nose, just before the world began to spin around and then disappear. The second was the ice cream I received while recovering. I was modestly disappointed in the fact that they delivered vanilla, when I had fervently hoped for chocolate. I was informed that this culinary gift was my reward for being a good boy. Finally, I recall the excitement brought about by the hemorrhage.

It all began on the seventh day, following the procedure. I was in our back yard, sitting on the deck of our pool, watching my older brother and his friends play. I must have become a little lightheaded because the next thing I knew I was underwater, fully clothed and heading for the bottom of the deep end. I had been taught, should I ever fall into the water by accident, to hold my breath and try to paddle to the edge of the pool. At that point, the last thing on my mind was escape. I was quite intrigued with the vision of my brother and his pals above me, swimming around a large float they had turned upside down and were using as a boat.

Drowning had not even crossed my mind. Suddenly my hero came down to get me and bring me back to the surface.

I got a bit of a scolding for my carelessness and my brother got a bit of ice cream, for saving my life and that was that; until just before midnight when I discovered the pillow beneath my head was covered in blood. A call was placed to our faithful surgeon, who drove the twenty miles from his home to ours, to cauterize the open wounds in my throat. Once out of danger, our man of medicine told me I was, *"A good little soldier!"* I also remember overhearing him tell my folks, *"That was a close one..."*

It was a strange and mysterious experience in my darkened room that night. As I drifted off to sleep, I realized that life was precious, health was a joy and my brother really did love me after all. I also learned that it's the little pauses 'tween the breaths that make life a wonder...

Tigger

Curious?

"*Curiouser* and *curiouser!*" cried Alice... Lewis Carroll, *Alice in Wonderland.* (1865) What a wonderful gift curiosity is. Even though I have a career, a four-generation family, and a journey upon which I have embarked, it is the little side trips that make this life so magnificent. Fifty-two times a year I return to my desk to create these Desert Wind Chronicles and each time I find myself digging into a subject that is new and fresh to me. Dictionaries, Google-aries, discussion-aries and remember-aries, all become a part of my continuing education. I want to know how, why, where, when and who, are the folks playing a part in the history of my stories.

It is not a journey through academia that inspires my adventure but rather the simple, joyful exploration of both big and little things that fire my imagination and fill my soul. I have written about the tiniest creatures, like bugs and butterflies. I have studied the biggest things, like galaxies and universes. I have contemplated invisible things, like thoughts and feelings and pondered that thing we call love. All of this because I am curious.

Have you ever met someone who acts like they know it all? I have and I'm always just as surprised as I was the first time. We all know stuff but none of us knows all the stuff. My parent's friends from Cal Tech were simply the most intelligent and knowledgeable people in the world. They knew about science and the astounding universe but had a tough time installing a diaper on their newborn. We all need to expand our knowledge and increase our wisdom. Curiosity is the best professor to accomplish this. Just ask Albert Einstein.

I believe that one of the great dangers of our nation and our world, is that so many of us have become convinced we know it all. We are so damn sure that we are right, we no longer feel intrigued or compelled to listen to the other guys point of view. You know the ancient expression, *"My mind is made up. Don't confuse me with the facts!"*

Tigger is a doctor of Lifeology, constantly growing, learning, expanding and trying to improve my me! I love you for sharing...

Tigger

The Instrument

During questions and answers at my Spiritsong Retreat, in Carmel California, one of our brilliant guests asked the following, *"If God played an instrument, what would it be?"* As I always try to do, I turned the question back to the attendees to hear their wisdom. *"A Trumpet,"* was the initial response. Her explanation was that august events are often preceded by a trumpet blast. In the case of Revelations, it is seven trumpet blasts that cue apocalyptic events. One gentleman in the audience suggested kettle drums. He pointed out that those powerful instruments are played to accentuate bigger than life movie scenes and commercials, in which size and grandeur need to be evoked. One other guest suggested that a cello might be the Lord's chosen instrument. It is soft, and sweet, yet very moving and powerful. Excellent answers I thought.

I recalled that, as a school child, if I waited long enough and looked down at the floor, no one would notice me, and I could avoid being called on. No such luck... *"Come on, Doug, what is your answer?"* As I try so hard to do, I had listened very carefully to the answers, rather than thinking of my response while others were speaking. I now had to gather my thoughts and wits about me. *"If God played an instrument what would it be?"* It was a well-crafted question and I thought it deserved a well thought out answer. My process: clear the decks of my mind, ask myself what

I think and then take it upstairs.

I believe that when we think of prayer, we often think of a long, deep, and ponderous effort. I love that type of meditative prayer, but I also genuinely enjoy asking for a brief conference with the almighty. *"Lord, if you were to choose a musical instrument to play, what would it be?"* The sweet, simple answer came back, *"A Flute!"*

Made sense to me. My thought was, breath is the gift of life. While it is present, we live, in its absence we die. As long as our breath is blown across and into a flute, the glorious, haunting sound lives. *He* breathes life into us, and our music becomes uplifting and wondrous.

I celebrate the chance to sit on the beach in Santa Barbara, California, and listen to my beloved friend Charles Lloyd breathe life into his beautiful composition, "Forest Flower…"

Tigger

The Key

Is there a key to happiness? How many times, since the dawn of history, has this question been asked and how many different responses have been offered? From religion, to love, to front row seats for your favorite performance, the answers are endless. Perhaps a better question is, *"Who holds this ancient wisdom?"* And the answer is, *"My wife does!"*

Sharon is a wonderful dancer. She is also a great speaker and perhaps just importantly, a long-time skater. Just this week I had the opportunity to watch her gliding around the rink, accompanied by our Canadian colleague Brian. With his bright red hockey jacket warming his broad shoulders, they cut a fine duo on the ice.

On our way back from the rink, our question of the key to happiness came up in the car and Sharon was quick to answer, *"The key to happiness lies on my dresser at home!"* As with one voice we asked and what pray-tell is this secret treasure? The answer came back as smooth as a crisp Triple-Lutz, *"My original skate key!"*

She began to recount the many sidewalks, streets and roller-skating rinks she had enjoyed, before switching to ice and becoming an accomplished figure skater. Just to keep it honest, she even threw in a couple of skinned knees along the way. What a joy to possess a treasure that opens the doorway to so many fond memories.

Have you ever gone skating? I have. In Watsonville, California, I remember a birthday skate with family and friends where we terrorized the floor for a whole warm California evening. Being a surfer boy, I never learned to ice skate, but I could roller rock and roll with the best of them.

From the sidewalks of Louisville, Kentucky, to a frozen lake in Vail, Colorado and now on the ice in Las Vegas, Nevada, the happiness goes on.

Skateaway...
Tigger

If It's Tuesday

The phone on my desk at KRLA Radio, beeped... It was Rosie our receptionist. *"Mr. Wolper is calling, and he would like to speak to you."* I must admit that I had no idea who Mr. Wolper was but I took the call. The soft- spoken caller explained that he (they) were casting a film and had chosen me to sing the theme song. Surprised? You bet! David Wolper explained that the crew at Wolper Productions (Willy Wonka), had put all the artists on UA records, into a pile and had chosen my voice as the right one for, "If It's Tuesday, this must be Belgium."

How this came to pass, is an amazing story of my good fortune. Donovan had written the song for the movie but could not perform it due to contractual conflicts. I find it humorous that he did perform and sing in the film but was not allowed to sing the theme. Lucky me.

I arrived to record my piece at the huge Hollywood studio. In the middle of the barn sized darkened building, I found a music stand, sheet music, a tall stool, a glass of water, a contract regarding my performance agreement and a beautiful Neuman Microphone. Through the studio window, I could see the director, Mr. Wolper and our musical director Walter Scharf. In my headset Mr. Wolper asked if I was ready. My response: *"Yep"* and we were rolling.

Through the window I saw for the first time, the scenes in the film that would accompany my song. I am good at preparation and so in one take it was done!

In Santa Barbara, California as we sat in our theater seats, the first scenes of the film began to roll and we heard the guitar and the song come through the theater speakers... *"If It's Tuesday, this must be Belgium..."* My young son jumped up on his seat and yelled, *"That's my dad singing!"* It was all the stardom I ever needed.

To share the song, do a Google search for J. P. Rags and If it's Tuesday this must be Belgium.

Tigger aka J.P. RAGS

Hugs

Outside, the fall wind and cold weather had finally arrived in our valley. Inside the warm auditorium, our annual Veteran's Day celebration had just concluded, and I was descending from the stage. What an honor to have been invited to share my gratitude with the Vet's, families, and friends in attendance and those beyond our view. My little part of the program was the reminiscence of a small boy, flag in hand, on the sidewalk during parades and in Pasadena's train station watching the troop trains roll through on their way to war.

At the bottom of the stairs, a charming lady, making way with her walker, pushed right up to me and asked, *"May I give you a hug?"* Like everyone who presents, whether in church or synagogue or in public, we want to know that we have fulfilled our charge and given a presentation worthy of the occasion. *"Of course,"* I replied. As this stranger and I embraced, I realized how fortunate we were to share this precious moment.

In this time of hatred, suspicion and division, in all corners of humanity, we had found a moment of unity. I was receiving the assurance that something I had said had been enjoyed and I was given the opportunity to embrace a stranger from our community.

I am aware that there are those who do not like to be hugged and

I honor their wishes. I will remember that Veteran's Day when, with tear-filled eyes, we shared our thanks for those who serve and those who care.

In Ashley Montague's book, *Touching: The Human Significance of the Skin,* he gives us something to think about as he reveals how human contact may just be a lifesaver for both children and adults.

How fortunate that this moment was experienced before the arrival of Covid-19. I wouldn't have missed it for the world!

Consider yourself hugged,
Tigger

The Timekeeper (Lichen)

"*How old do you think that boulder is,*" the ranger asked? "*One Year? One Thousand Years? One Million Years?*" We had hiked to the top of Buena Vista Peak, in King's Canyon National Park, on a guided adventure. Walking through the incense cedars, pines, and manzanita, crossing the carpet of mustang clover and blue-eyed Mary blossoms, we made our way to the summit. From the top, we could look out onto Redwood Mountain Grove, the world's largest remaining stand of giant sequoias. It was a fragrant carpet of huge treetops.

Our eyes feasting on the colors, our noses dancing on the fragrance of the sweet environment created by the giants and our better angels realizing that we were viewing what might well be the last of a species. "Dendrology," they call it. The science and study of wooded plants. On the top of the world, we were a handful of witnesses to a marvelous history.

As our small group gathered around our guide, he explained that this part of his presentation was to bring our attention to the map-like material growing on the giant boulders surrounding us. We learned that these colorful patches were Lichen, some of the earth's oldest organisms. My interest was piqued, because on the way up Doug's Mountain, in Nevada, I find these beautiful blue, green and white patches decorating the boulders along *my* pathway. Ranger Dick explained that the presence of Lichen and the size of the patches on the boulders, was an indicator of how long ago the rock face was uncovered.

When the appropriate moment arose for questions, I asked, *"How can I approximate the age of the material that surrounds the pathway up my trail?"* From his response it seems that the rocks and boulders along my path were spewed there by a volcano about fifteen-million-years ago and the lichens thereon are probably 500-1000 years old. We were a blessed group of humanity seeing and breathing in a moment of time, a moment that may never come again.

Happy Birthday, Earth!

Ranger in training...
Tigger

The Web

Have you ever looked at the computer screen in front of you and cursed the day it was invented? Have you ever been enjoying a meal in a restaurant or a hike in the country and received an unwanted call on your cell phone? *"I'd like to throw this thing in the lake!"* you exclaim. Me too, but then this happens: A truly dear friend of many years, posts a photo on Facebook and you feel instantly connected, transported, warmed, and inspired.

The photo I describe was a gift from my dear friend, colleague and brother, Wayne Grund. Wayne is a proud Canadian with "world citizen" rightfully added to his title. I have had the blessing of standing on stage with this bright, energetic performer on many occasions. One of the things I admire most about the magic Mr. Grund is that he would often join me in the audience before and after our performances, to celebrate and learn from our fellow performers and educators.

On one of his many family visits to Kipabiscau Lake, in Saskatchewan, he captured a magical photo of a morning spider web in the mist. It is a treasure to me, because it reminds me of how the thread of an idea is captured and woven, by those who believe, into a piece of artwork and beauty that shimmers like diamonds in the morning light.

Such is the story of Wayne's Company, "Surface Hair." From an idea and a dream in 2008, to a major force, creating, educating, and inspiring a whole new generation of professionals and their clients, I give a cheer!

Those of us who have eyes, can see through the gossamer web, the pathway to the realization of the dream. As a very *Brave* Viking princess followed a wisp to her mystical adventure, we can find our way to a new world of success.

Is it time to start your own wonder?

Thank you, my friend...
Tigger

Sunlight

The year was 1969, a time for great causes and great music. As program Director for KRLA, it was my responsibility to find and program the best music possible. As I shared with Casey Kasem, his first day on the air, if you love those people out there in southern California, they will love you right back. The "Kaser" kept this promise and boy did Southern California love him back!

One bright morning in my office on the Huntington Hotel campus, my friend from RCA records handed me a "45" (That's a small circular piece of black vinyl, with a hole the size of a silver dollar in the middle) with the words, *"You're gonna love this one Cox..."* As I always tried to do, I dropped the needle and listened to his record. *"Love is but a song we sing and fear's the way we die..."* Jesse Colin Young's voice was sweet and gentle, and the lyrics were powerful. With those two opening lines he had me. They sang out everything that our station stood for.

When I told the promotion man, we were going to program his song, he was overjoyed. Up until that moment, he confessed, nobody in our market had chosen to play it. When I made this commitment, I had no idea what I was getting into. We played "Get Together," by the Youngbloods for the next nine months, with a great response from our intelligent, caring audience but few if any went to a record shop to buy a copy. Up until that moment, airplay was based on sales and as my boss said, *"They ain't buying it!"* I risked my job and said we need to keep this message on the air. I begged my world-war- two-gruff manager, to listen through to the end and he did so.

By the time the song ended, Hal agreed to let me keep the ride going. Some things are worth the risk! *"We are but a moment's Sunlight fading in the grass."* We helped make it a hit and I found the inspiration for a book title.

Tigger

Lead

It is *"end-of-summer-hot"* on Doug's Mountain. Heading down from the summit on a fine morning, Las Vegas lies out below me, like an alabaster city. From up here you can't see them but on that strip, there are two hundred thousand guests and a host of locals to bid them welcome, serve their meals and deal their cards. Behind the cement and neon of our exciting and vibrant city, stands the Spring Mountains, an eight-thousand-foot cathedral to the Great Spirit. This is a wonderful place to live and share.

Coming up the trail toward me, is a sight that I enjoy, a family. How I love this; the father up ahead and two boys in tow. Just a guess but they are perhaps eight and ten years of age and they are strung out behind their dad, with a four-foot space between them. I say a simple, cheerful, *"Howdy,"* to the dad in the lead and he, without looking up, grunts an unintelligible sound. As he passes, I speak to his lads, *"Good Morning men!"* They, without looking up, offer a grunt to match their father's salutation.

As they switchback above me, I hear the dad ask, *"Why didn't you speak to that man back there?"* Their response? *"You told us not to speak to strangers!"*

It has taken a number of years for me to get it, but I am beginning to understand that the attitudes and actions of other folks that cross our paths have been formed over a lifetime of observation, experience, and personal involvement. If I don't smile, there is a very good chance that my family did not smile either. If I shy away from a hug, it may just be that my dad was not a hugger and I sure wanted to be a man just like him.

Someone is always watching us. How we act, react, and treat others, is always laying the psychological groundwork for the those who come under our influence.

Which is it, Dad? Lead, follow or get out of the way!

Tigger

Flight #565

Somewhere between Denver and Detroit, the announcement came, *"Ladies and gentlemen, this is your captain speaking. I am sad to announce that our founder and chairman emeritus, Herb Kelleher, has passed away."* Not the words that one might expect to hear over the P.A. on a Boeing seven-thirty- seven at 35,000 feet.

If the words were a surprise, the reaction was not. The loss of a leader is always a shock but the passing of this beloved man, opened the floodgates. As the skipper continued to reveal the depth of affection the team-members of Southwest felt for their C.E.O., the flight attendants were in tears and those who were Rapid Rewards Regulars were visibly shaken.

The captain continued to reveal that "Herb's" drink of choice had always been Wild Turkey bourbon and that everyone on board was invited to raise a cup, take a sip and celebrate a leader whose creative genius, business acumen, courage, sense of humor and love for his people and company was unparalleled.

During the process of creating a historical document for our company I did a thorough search of the rhymes and reasons for the incredible success of Southwest Airlines. Needless to say, the name of the founder, Herb Kelleher, was a constant thread in the story.

My dear friend and close associate in the executive strata at Hard Rock International is David Carroll. In his highly successful career, Vice President of Southwest Airlines stood out on his resume. In our discussions whenever the name Herb Kelleher came up, there was a look in David's eyes that said, *"Great leader, great man!"*

Here's to you Herb… May all who choose to lead others, observe well and do their best to emulate this wonderful man, whose connection to his people and his company was so great, that his passing brought both tears for our loss and cheers for his contribution to our travels.

Tigger

Dialect

I love language. Whether it is the species humanus or other wild critters, I am entranced by the sounds and inflections of voices, calls and songs. That is why when I came to live in the desert of the Southwest, I was more excited than ever to get out among 'em, tune in and converse with the locals.

During my life along the California Coast of America, I had developed an unusual skill. I was and am very proud of my ability to communicate with critters, in particular, Valley quail. I love their familiar *"Chiquita-Chiquita,"* song and I knew that adding a voice to the joy of watching them, would be a wonder.

Once, in the parking lot of the luxurious Ventana hotel and spa, on the cliff overlooking the grand Pacific Ocean, I was trying out my newly acquired skill of chatting with quail. I had been practicing with my trusty Lohman quail call, on the streets and in the gardens of my beloved Carmel and had some success on making contact with these beauties, so I was ready. I stood entranced by the view and fragrance of the wild and wonderful brush below me. I listened quietly and carefully, until I heard the call and then I responded, *"Chiquita-Chiquita!"* I only presented twice and up over the crest of the hill at my feet, appeared a fine covey of beautiful quail!

Having thus received my doctorate in quail-ology, I felt very well prepared and qualified to head into the desert and reach out to my new friends. Watching a gathering of Gambel's quail, on our monastery desert-scape, I raised my call to my lips. *"Good morning new friends! I'm Doug Cox from California and I wanted to say howdy!"* I'm not sure how my tones translated but at the sound of my call, the covey exploded and disappeared into the desert chaparral. Dialect! I needed to work on my dialect!

Tigger

Frantic (Part One)

The thunderstorms around Denver were mighty; mighty tall and mighty powerful. Our little 737 was no match. Here's the deal. We were flying into DIA to land and connect with our next flight. So, the fact that our silver bird was being tossed around like a kitten in a clothes-dryer, didn't set an encouraging tone for our timely arrival and departure.

Once in the terminal, I headed from gate 26 to gate 36 and took my seat to await our delayed flight. While seated I noticed a young lady pacing back and forth. She appeared to be a Colorado Native. Her attire screamed, *"Climb the Rockies"* and her oversized backpack was not one for the weak. Yet here in the airport of John Denver, she was acting crazed.

When the storms passed and we were invited to board, it reminded me of my friend Hadley Barrett, the great rodeo announcer who used to say when commenting on a cowboy who was mercilessly bucked off a monster bull, only to be granted a re-ride. (Who would want one?) I found my favorite seat in the front row next to the window. It just seemed that this should be a terrific re-ride over the Rockies and home to Las Vegas, when through the aircraft doorway appeared the mountain lassie. She paused in the doorway, as if deciding whether to come in or turn around and run. Once inside she looked wild-eyed at the two of us in the front row and stammered out, *"Is that center seat taken?"* The answer was no ma'am and welcome aboard.

As she flopped into the seat beside me, she simply burst into tears and started shrieking, *"I've already had three flights canceled, my backpack is never going to fit up there and I am never going to make it to San Francisco!"*

Stay tuned for the rest of this crazy story!
Tigger

Frantic (Part Two...)

The young lady was still crying, face down in her hands, when my seatmate and I leaned forward to try to connect and console our new arrival. He, sitting on the aisle, is a Vietnam Vet. I see this by his proudly worn cap and I, sitting at the window, am an appreciative civilian. We have unwittingly been presented with a thoroughly distraught backpacker. Just as she draws in a deep breath between sobs, our angel arrives.

From the seat directly behind us, I catch a glimpse of a Southwest Uniform. It is our mid-cabin flight attendant and she, having observed the activity, knows that a disturbed person on a flight, is a bad and perhaps dangerous thing. She speaks and her voice is both kind and authoritative. *"May I help you stow your backpack?"* The agitated passenger waves her off as if to say, *"Don't touch me,"* and the FA* continues in the very same kind voice, *"I am here to make sure that you are comfortable..."* This exceptional choice of words seemed to turn the tide and our freaked-out neighbor finally responded, *"Ok."*

I share this with my readers, because it was an example of guest service at the very highest level. Our angel had been observing the boarding process, instead of discussing her personal life or the airline schedule with another flight attendant and saw the potential human-storm gathering. She listened and instead of challenging the distraught lady about her backpack on the floor, she offered to assist. Finally, she shared the one thing that we all need when we are lost, confused and stressed, *"I am here to make sure that you are comfortable..."* Next time things come apart in the department store, school or church, remember our angel; observe, listen and speak to comfort your neighbor.

The once frantic passenger even laughed with Tigger on the flight! (*Flight Attendant/Angel)

Grandpa's Kite

Our grandpa's workshop always smelled like magic to this little boy. Surrounded by split-oak, eucalyptus and cedar wood, the fireplace logs lay drying in stacks, seasoning for the fire that would warm our winter home. It was a place of wonder, because in my grandfather's hands, bits of wood and pieces of string always became something special.

On one fine sunny California morning, grandpa had an excited air about him, as he took me by the hand and led me out to the workshop. *"Dougal,"* he said, *"today we are going to make a kite!"* After all these years I can still remember feeling the excitement in the old man's hand.

As he often did, during our adventures, he used our time together to share his wisdom and prepare me for my own grand-fathership one day. As he turned the beautiful sheets of crepe paper, balsa sticks and string into a colorful flying machine, he explained… *"A kite is very much like a dream. It begins as a picture in our minds but through our imagination, patience and labors, it becomes real."*

In the meadow, out past the barn, I watched that colorful piece of artwork lift-off into the afternoon breeze, where it began to dance in the bright blue sky. It was such a joy to watch grandpa let out the string and see the kite become smaller and smaller as it was heaven bound. I couldn't wait for my turn to hold the dream, and once in my hands I was devastated when my concentration slipped, and I let the ball of string slip away. As I chased after the bouncing ball just ahead of my stumbling feet, I finally gave up and realized that in an instant our beautiful kite, was gone.

The lesson was clear. Hold tight to your dreams or they may well disappear into the blue sky of in-attention. I loved my Grandpa beyond imagination!

Tigger

Circle of Concern

The little red Volkswagen was broadsided by a racing Ford Mustang. The *VW* driver was severely injured. As the witnesses began running around throwing their hands in the air and screaming, I walked to the side of the rolling vehicle and steered it away from the cliff, for which it was headed. I comforted the injured driver, by assuring her that she would be alright and awaited the ambulance.

I have always been a soft-hearted character. In the early days of my speaking career, the authority that stage presence offers, (for real or imagined) brought audience members to ask for guidance with their problems. I have never been a counselor. I have always been a cowboy with the experience that age brings.

I did make a discovery early on, that helped me not only survive but be of some support and strength for those in turmoil and pain. My first reaction to an emotional outreach, was to rush in and get involved in the situation. What I quickly found was, the moment I became sympathetically involved I was as angry, hurt, sick, confused and as lost as the soul who had requested my support.

Since this discovery, I have made it a point to stand outside of the circle of concern remaining as calm as possible, focused, strong, ready, and able to support. Empathy has a power to give strength and guidance, that sympathy cannot. Do not misunderstand... On that roadway, in Hurricane, Utah, my heart was racing.

I am deeply touched by what happens to those around me and was honored to be invited to the hospital to visit with the victim and her family, my new friends.

You can decide to do this too.
Tigger

Bloom

"Isn't it awful!" The exasperated voice on the other end of my smartphone, was a longtime dear friend. She sounded simply devastated...

The politics of our once faithful and committed nation has been reduced to calling names and trying to bring each other crashing down, instead of lifting one another up. Now the invasion of the coronavirus. *"It's just too much,"* she exclaimed. I feel these emotions too, but I have a little voice inside me that faithfully whispers, *"Look around, can't you find some possibilities?"*

As a wildlife photographer, I have captured more than ten-thousand flower photos. What I have learned from this joyful experience is, that however long the day or how hopeless the search has been, there is always a fresh vision, a new floral wonder just ahead. On this day, my miracle appeared just before me on the dusty trail. A tiny desert butterfly led the way and I came upon a Sphaeralcea emoryi, or as I call it, Emory's globemallow.

That is how, in the midst of this medical calamity and these days of uncivil discourse, I have discovered on the doorstep of springtime, the first bloom of hope. My Native American friends and guides taught me long ago, to walk gently on the earth in winter, for she is pregnant with the spring. Wherever our minds go and whatever dark corners we may find there, this mysterious world of ours, is always preparing itself to spring forth with new life.

Trapped in our negative, frightened and frightening thoughts, we cannot possibly find the courage and strength to help rescue the drowning around us. Faith and fear cannot live in the same house. It is only in the springtime of our own minds and thoughts, that we will find the strength to see to the blossoming of our fellow citizens, sisters and brothers.

One bloom is proof positive that this too shall pass.

I'm a believer...
Tigger

Burbank

I love it. I am always excited when I see the letters BUR printed on my airline ticket. Wherever I am coming from, BUR means that I am heading toward the place of so many of my life's performances. It was here that I began in earnest, my speaking career and did I mention it's the home of Walt Disney Headquarters?

It's a mere forty-five bumpy minutes from our Las Vegas airport, (LAS) to the Burbank Airport, in Southern California (BUR). What a wonderful, romantic place it is. Nestled in the Sierra Madre mountains, it is truly the airport of the stars.

For eighty-nine years, the likes of Bogart and Bacall, Marylin Monroe, Clint Eastwood, Burt Reynolds, John Travolta, Jake Gyllenhaal, Tim Burton, Paul McCartney, Jay Leno and of course the late great namesake of the airport, Bob Hope, have arrived and or departed here. In the many years I have been a traveler through this storied airport, I have never walked the departure lounge, without seeing a celebrity.

There is a wonderful myth heard at Hollywood cocktail parties, that the touching, romantic airport scene concluding the film, Casa Blanca, was filmed at the Burbank Airport. Bring it up in the presence of the cognoscenti and you will get an earful from both sides. A passenger who touches down at Burbank, is in driving distance to the best of Southern California attractions, like The Hollywood Bowl, The Walk of Fame, Hollywood and Vine, Warner Brothers, Disney, Paramount, and Universal Studios, where you can go behind the scenes and enjoy insider access to movie making secrets.

Whether it was my first flight in a DC-3, my joyful teenage ride in a Constellation or yesterday's flight in a Southwest 737, the journey to and through Bob Hope International Airport, was and is a ride on a Hollywood magic carpet.

All Aboard...
Tigger

Coach

I do not watch football for political commentary. I watch football on television because it is a sport I really enjoy. I also watch because once long, long ago, in a high school far-far away, I played the game with great joy. My coach was a fine, straight ahead fellow named, Walt Smith. Walt was a no-nonsense guy when it came to both his players and the game. So, one warm California afternoon when he called me to the bench, I hustled over and sat down in anticipation.

"Cox!" he said in his husky voice, *"Do you like this?"* Not sure what he was asking about, I responded *"Like what, sir?" "Sitting here on this bench?"* I still didn't get it. I knew that being the littlest kid on the team, I was being used as a tackling dummy by players, all of whom were much bigger than me. He went on to ask me, as good coaches do, why I played football and why I hung in there, considering my place in the pecking order. Although I knew it sounded like I was opening a common can of answers, I responded that I loved the game. I also mentioned that there was a certain young lady sitting in the stands on whom I wanted, (more than anything) to make a favorable impression. *"Then you don't want to be sitting out here,"* he said, as he motioned to the field. *"You want to be playing in there!"* Of course, he was right. *"How?"* I asked.

"You must do three things you are not doing now. First you need to play with your eyes open, looking for opportunities. Second you need to play with your mind open. You may not be bigger than the other guys but you sure are smarter!" "But won't I get hurt out there?" I asked. "Probably," he answered, "but not if you play wide open. It's simple power math. The faster and more committed you are in your actions, the less likely you are of being hurt." To this day I still play the game of life and business with my eyes open and mind open - wide open!

Aside from the fact that I got my front tooth kicked out, recovering a game winning fumble, I played football safely and joyously through high school.

I also attended the prom with that certain young lady. Thanks Coach...

Tigger #22

Solid Gold

Everyone that I have ever met likes at least *some* kind of music. Imagine what a joy it was to have music as a major part of my career. As you read through these stories and share with us the energy and celebration of my seminars, you will begin to feel the thrill and the emotion pour out. This is one story about an incredibly special day in my life as a record promotion man.

Twenty-Five-Twenty-Five West Ninth Street, in Los Angeles, was a historic building. It was the place I first met Smokey Robinson, Stevie Wonder, Otis Redding, Marvin Gaye, Tammi Terrell and Wilson Pickett. Merit Distributing was the sales and promotion point for the hottest record companies in the world. Atlantic/ATCO, Stax-Volt, Motown, Tamla, Chess, Checker, Argo and the beat goes on. We Were Hot Stuff!

One morning, when we were sipping coffee, trying to get our day started, something happened that shook our world and the world of entertainment forever. Eddie, the man who ran the sales floor downstairs, often played records to introduce us to the latest release on one of our great labels. It was our version of a three-minute sales meeting. This time it was a game changer...

The rhythm, the voice, the band, the singers and the lyrics, stopped us all in our tracks! *"What you want... Baby I got it!"* It filled the building and went straight through our being and into our DNA. We were cheering, dancing and clapping. We knew the "Queen of Soul" was being born.

Aretha Franklin was and always will be a one-of-a-kind solid gold star. I was fortunate to help promote her and her recordings on the west coast. Her gospel roots were not left behind. As incredibly gifted a performer as she was, she was also a kind, gentle and a thankful human being to me.

It was my honor to have known "The Queen of Soul!"

R.E.S.P.E.C.T.
Tigger

Furry and Feathered Family

Have you ever watched a newscast and found yourself overwhelmed by the complexity and challenges of our times? Me too! While watching the "telly" in our home, when the little red recording light comes on, you can bet that we are capturing something special to watch at a later date and time.

Our southern Mother, who loved the outdoors and the critters therein, brought with her, from McMinnville, Tennessee, some mighty colorful expressions... Fixin', Catawampus, Yonder, Doohickey, Hissy, Druthers and of course, Bless your heart! These here are all goodern's, but my favorite will always be *kin!* I love the word because it means *family*...

It is also the name of my new friend Kin Quituga, who along with two associates, in 1986 founded HawkQuest, a Colorado Non-Profit charitable Organization, for the purpose of rescuing and sharing raptors with the world.

Kin and HawkQuest believe that by introducing these marvelous birds of prey to the public, in a fun and educational way, they can impress upon people of all ages, the importance of preserving ecosystems and the wildlife that depends upon them.

Kin has found a great way for us to share in the wellbeing of the "fowls of the air." To become contributors and caretakers of these beautiful hawks, eagles, owls, and falcons, each of us has the opportunity to play a part in fulfilling our stewardship with these regal creatures. Kinfolk with wings!

There is a very valid reason why so many of us are attracted to and entranced by animal shows on television. Whether it is nature in the raw or veterinarians trying to save the lives and limbs of all critters large and small, we love our animal families and the ratings prove my point.

Check out the HawkQuest website (www.hawkquest.org) and add to your knowledge and your wardrobe, with their beautiful T-shirts and Sweatshirts.

Tigger

Honest

He came to us as so many had before... A young, talented singer and songwriter. Of course, we wanted to help everyone of them become a star, but we knew that was not the reality. We always listened patiently and carefully to new artists, the performance, the song and the back story.

Bobby was a gentleman; a handsome young fellow who told a good story. He had a song idea that was different and intriguing and a fine voice and style. We agreed to help him put out his first record, "Walking Together." In our recording studio, we brought in a great band, turned on the mics, turned down the lights and produced this record.

Although we had our own record label, we felt it best for Bobby, that we offer his record to a company more established than our own. We chose Moonglow Records, on which the Righteous Brothers and many other stars had produced hits. The label was owned by a man named Art Laboe, founder of the world-renowned, *Oldies but Goodies* label. Art liked our production and agreed to release "Walking Together," on Moonglow Records.

I tell you all of this because, as it is with a new artist, most of the world never heard Bobby's performance. The exception was Hawaii. For some reason the islands liked Bobby's song. Radio stations played it and people bought it. If you know the record business, you are aware that getting played and getting sold are a long way from getting payed.

We were so thrilled with the airplay and the sales, that we never thought about getting payed, but the great Art Laboe, a dear friend, and a fine and honest man, sent us a check for our Hawaiian record sales. ($136.00)

Diogenes' lamp revealed an honest soul after all!
Tigger

(You can share our record by doing a Google search for Bobby Mac and "Walking Together.")

Changing of the Guard

We who are born into an inquisitive, interested family are truly blessed. We are constantly exposed to people and places that others may never hear or wonder about. My dad brought with him from England, his own story of the changing of the guard at Buckingham Palace. The telling of which, in his beautiful British accent, in the light and warmth of our woodfire, included the reading of A. A. Milne's *Buckingham Palace*. Not to be outdone, we here in the desert have our own version of this wonder.

In the predawn darkness, the air is still, the desert wind is at peace and the parade begins. As the last echoes of the poorwills sing, *"Poor-Will-Up, Poor-Will-Up..."* the song-dogs (coyotes) grab the baton and take up the chorus. *"Yip-Yip-Awooooo!"* It is another glorious sunrise, in the mysterious, beautiful southwestern desert.

As the great horned owl departs the trees behind our home and takes wing up to her nest on the cliffs above us, the beautiful gambel's quail begin their quest for attention, *"Chiquita-Chiquita..."* they sing. It won't be long before we see, in the gathering light, a wonderful quail's parade of parents leading their babies, scampering along like furry golf balls with legs, better than any cartoon! How appropriate that the quail found in the desert outside Las Vegas, are so named Gambels!

Next is the male mockingbird, who, having found no mate, begins to call in desperation. Then, precisely at six A.M, in the distance, we hear the first commercial flight from our airport, as the captain pushes the throttle forward and gathers speed along runway 8L/26R. Southwest #2358 is headed for Denver and the sounds of the outside world join in.

From the voices of one creature to the next, such are the sights and sounds of the daily changing of the guard at our monastery. Each voice wakes up a different treasure every morning, a sweet surprise.

I am ready for a camp-out... How' bout you?
Tigger

Making the Grade

Like the cover art from a mystery novel, it draws me in. The Martin Grade, whose golden opening to twelve miles of tree sheltered roadway, running from the Atlantic Ocean to the shores of one of the largest lakes in America, is a wonder.

For most of the tree lined odyssey, the blue Florida sky above, is obscured by a cathedral of branches. Standing as a remnant of Florida's past, one- hundred-year-old Southern Live Oaks, Birch and Maple, begrudgingly allow patches of sunlight through, to dance on the roadway beneath me.

"The Grade," as locals call it, leads to one of my favorite places in the world, the Reservation of The Seminole Tribe of Florida, and the mighty Brighton Casino in the heart of the everglades. I am writing about it in this edition, because this is Labor Day and I am honored to say, I just spent the last three days with Marty Johns, the General Manager and his courageous, bright and committed leadership team, preparing for a very exciting and prosperous future.

Marty is the son of Josiah Johns, one of the greatest Indian cowboys of all time and an inductee into the Indian National Finals Rodeo Hall of Fame. One evening, on the way home, after a rodeo performance, Marty's dad and mom were killed by a drunk driver. Suddenly, this young cowboy found himself responsible for helping the struggling business survive and grow. He and his team have done both. The Brighton Casino is a shining light in the properties of the Seminole Tribe in Florida.

Besides the people and the fried chicken at Josiah's Restaurant, something wonderful is cooking at the Mighty Brighton. You might just want to head down "The Grade" toward the Casino in the Everglades. I will meet you there!

Cowboy Tigger

Friends

Have you ever walked along street in your town only to find yourself confronted by a homeless person? What do you think? What do you do? What do you say? At first, we doubt the ragged soul before us. Why doesn't he just get a job? Why doesn't she get into one of those shelters?

And then we begin to question ourselves. I would like to give them a few dollars but if I did that for every homeless person who approaches me, I would be homeless too... What should I do?

Imagine with me if you can: The weather has turned cold and windy. You are shivering and hungry. The few ragged pieces of clothing with which you wrap your gaunt frame, are no match for the frigid desert afternoon. Fifteen minutes away by car, people are laughing, drinking, dining and gambling in the brightly lit casinos of Las Vegas. You are homeless.

It is four P.M and you are waiting in line for what may be the only meal you will have today. At five P.M the sanctuary door will close and lock behind you. Not locked to keep people out but locked to keep the decorum of the service and the moments of peace and fellowship, intact. If you are hungry, sober and able, you are inside and ready for a blessing and a hot meal.

The "Friends in the Desert" are at it again, serving the less fortunate of our community. Homeless and hungry, often hard working and simply unable to keep up with the cost of survival in our privileged nation, they have come out from the shadows, to find sustenance for another solitary night.

I write about this very real place, because we have recently had the opportunity to be a contributor to the cause. As members of our Variety Club of neighbors and friends, we created and produced a Holiday Performance with the intention of sharing the proceeds of our ticket sales.

Here's to all our neighbors and friends who performed in or attended the show and to the volunteer/servants contributing to the hopeful part of our community. *"Another day for you and me in paradise..."* (Phil Collins)

Bless you Friend,
Tigger

"A"

A is for ask: Before he came to us, he had been a law enforcement officer with a perfect record. He was a respected leader on the force and noted for his attention to detail in his work. G.K. was looked up to, by his fellow officers. In his professional life he had been a counselor and a teacher.

A is for Ambassador: Because that's what he became to us. When I needed someone to help connect our Coconut Creek property, to our corporate team in Hollywood, he was assigned to me. Even if he wasn't always the first to understand, he was always the first to raise his hand and jump in to do his part. His approach and demeanor helped to build the spirit of the project. I trusted him.
A is for Aloha: I remember the first time I overheard someone who worked with him say, *"Oh him, he's just stupid!"* I felt like I had been shot. As the days, weeks and months passed by, he began to struggle with even the simplest of tasks. We provided each of our Ambassadors with an inexpensive but fine camera, to capture the special adventures happening on their respective properties. G.K. had a struggle loading the batteries and turning on his camera. He could not email the photos to us. Then I heard it again, *"The guy's just an idiot!"*

A is for Alzheimer's: That is the disease that took our friend from us in the middle of the night.

A is for always: Always be aware of the good in others. Look for the best, not the worst. We all have challenges. I might list a few of those who never wavered: A brother, president, boss, a cop, and an angel who put me on the phone with my dear friend during the last days of his life. G. K.'s true friends were faithful till the end.

We Ride Together...
Tigger

Hero (RIP Papa)

I received a touching, inspiring email from our neighbor this morning. Her words reached into my heart and soul and sparked this question in my mind: *How would we choose to celebrate a hero of our days? What words set down, would honor the power of his ways?*

Perhaps a daughter's loving expression captures it best. *"My Dear Father,"* her letter began... Perhaps the foundation word that best describes a hero, (or shero) as I call them, is "loved." Not for big things done occasionally but for little things done faithfully and consistently, throughout a lifetime.

"My Papa was a hero, in every sense of the word," her letter continues: then let us add courageous to the words of tribute and description. *"As a World War II prisoner of war survivor, three and a half years in captivity and survival from two of the Hell ships,"* her statement leaves no doubt.

Her writing makes it clear that no description of a hero would be complete, without the word "Romantic..." *"His eternal optimism and desire to survive so he could marry my mother, his one and only, kept him going."* When there is a why, we can overcome any what.

As her thoughts on paper flowed, I could see this man and feel her reverence for him: *"My Papa was super down-to-earth, humble and loyal. He loved nature, especially birds and trees; his glass was always full, no half-ways!"*

And finally, might we add the word *"Grateful..."* Like papa, like daughter...

What a joy it is, at whatever time of year, to walk out into our street and give a wave to the daughter of our hero or to share a holiday glass of wine and some fine conversation with our own hero, Mary.

Tigger

A Gift (Packages)

"*Packages...*" Boy do we love them! We even have a funny way of pronouncing the word. A package in a mail person's hand, the arrival a UPS truck or an Amazon vehicle on our street, was and is a cause for youthful anticipation. Back in the day, on our farm, I heard my mom and dad talk over exactly what we needed and then write a letter to "Monkey Ward" or "Sear's Sawbuck," and then we would wait. Recently I realized I needed something. It was an item that I could not make. Something I could not find in a local store, an item that to me would be a treasure.

I needed a way to transport my new iPhone everywhere I went, through airports, on horseback, onstage and certainly climbing Doug's Mountain. I knew that this device must be sturdy, custom fitted so as not to risk loss, easily positioned and of course, great looking.

Enter my wonderful friend, Mike Clifford. Not only is Mike a healer, philosopher, world class fly-fisherman but he is a leather crafter, par excellence. So, I called him in Texas and patiently described the object of my desires. He very kindly offered to create a holster for my smarter-than-me phone. He did just that! In a couple of weeks, as it has been since the dawn of time I imagine, there it was... a package on my porch.

Mike's creation, which I wear nearly every moment of the day, reminded me that a gift, like a friend, is most celebrated, when it possesses these four things:

    1. It should be something that the recipient needs!
    2. It should be serviceable, of use daily and long lasting!
    3. It must be suitable to the recipient's style and fashion!
    4. It must be created/purchased and presented with love and respect!

Next time I am planning on sharing a gift, I am going to use what I learned from Mike and follow the checklist above to assure maximum enjoyment. Each time I reach for my phone, I will remember and appreciate my friend.

Now... where did I put that phone?
Tigger

Sentinel Species...

Do you appreciate a timely and honest warning of approaching danger? I do. Sentinel Species are animals used to detect risk to humans, by providing advanced warnings of danger. I remember when I was a kid, the word passed through the newspaper I delivered, that something mysterious was killing off America's bald eagles. I loved eagles then, as I do now and word that the population of those regal symbols of our nation were in danger of disappearing, sent a chill through my little boy-scout being.

Our scientist friend explained that farmers had been using a chemical called DDT and our abuse of this chemical was the culprit. Today we know that many creatures have given us a forewarning of chemical and environmental factors, that have endangered us humans.

Turns out, as you know, that eagles were not the first. During the California gold rush, miners carried caged canaries into the mines, to alert them of poisonous air in the shafts. In the 1950s the Japanese noticed that cats in the town Minamata, Japan had begun acting strangely. At first, they had a hard time walking and then they began jumping about uncontrollably. This mercury-induced "Dancing Cat Fever" behavior eventually appeared in the town's people. Head's up!

Our list of sentinel species now includes polar bears, dolphin and my beloved honeybees. Researchers are attaching microsensors to bees, to assess their ability to pollinate. My newest favorite is the device attached to a drone, used to "snatch snot samples" from a whale's blowhole at sea, to determine their wellbeing. What did *"you"* do at the office today?

We truly need to be aware of how environmental changes effect our wellbeing and longevity.

I'm watching,
Tigger

Let's Ride

Have you got a partner with whom you make beautiful music? The one who, whatever the time of day or night, has never said no to an invitation. Well I sure do! We've seen some wonderful places together and ridden through some exotic climes. In fact, she is sitting right out there in the driveway now. I call her the "silver bullet," in honor of the Lone Ranger...

I am not sure about you but as the years go by, I always think that I will get bored or tired of my stuff. It just has not happened. Somewhere, deep inside of me, there is a teenage boy trying to get out. It's something about young men, their dreams, and their cars.

It all began when I was in the record business. I had put my heart and soul into getting airplay on some "hard-to-break" recordings. Once they made it over the wave and onto the playlists of some big-time radio stations, my boss called me in and said, *"Job well done my man, go pick out a car."* I did just that and a show-room new GTO was the beginning of my addiction. I was now driving my reward car from Atlantic Records.

My second experience came, when I had moved on to radio and it was time to turn in the Pontiac. In those days you could lease a used auto. My friend in the leasing biz, called to tell me he had a big-time radio-TV guy, who leased a new buggy every two years and turned the old one in with less than ten-thousand miles on it. A two-year-old Cadillac with low miles was a prize, so I took it. That gun-metal 1969 caddy, was the first of four cars I picked up, from the great Gary Owens.

I used to think that it was a guy thing, but I know plenty of ladies who love cars. Just ask my wife, as she climbs into her custom-purple, 1999 Jeep Classic, to head out to her dance class.

So here we are, sixty years later and our terrific neighbor is guiding us in the process of stepping into that "new car smell" once again. May I suggest a ride up P.C.H., that's Pacific Coast Highway to you inlanders.

We Ride Together,
Tigger

Ruby Rapidamente

Rapidamente: *Quickly, Rapidly, Fast...* That is how everything happens in the southwestern desert. From the birth of a cactus blossom, to its passing, may be as brief as two days. Even the tiny iridescent creature that we know as a ruby-throated hummingbird, has a valiant heart that beats twelve- hundred-sixty times a minute. From our Nevada monastery, he takes wing in autumn and heads for south America. Traveling the same route year after year, he returns to the same ocotillo or feeder in springtime, often flying for 500 miles without stopping.

My faithful readers know that over the years, we have lost two young members of our family. Our daughter Barbee left us many years ago and our grandson Danny crossed the bridge recently. Our romantic and loving family has found ways to hold them close as time goes by. Barbee's ashes, at her request, were scattered in the Pacific Ocean, that she might continue surfing with us. Danny, we have decided, comes to us in the form of a hummingbird. You can imagine how we anticipate his return each spring.

If you are a hummingbird feeder enthusiast please, follow the rules. Your gardening store can guide you on the flowers that best nourish your friends. A hummer feeder is a supplemental source for your tiny treasures. A super clean feeder with a 1:4 solution of tap water and refined white sugar is the best. No coloring in the water. The key is proper cleaning, so during the summer twice a week is best. Hot tap water and a weak vinegar solution. No soaps!

With tiny wings that beat eighty times a second, these proud spirit creatures fly all alone, carrying our love and admiration south, to our Familia-del-sur and then, well fed and rested, they carry the spirit of our loved ones back home to us.

Hold your loved ones close... Life is brief and passes Rapidamente!

Love,
Tigger

Windows

The best way to see a place is to walk… What do you think? On our recent national seminar tour, when labor and lectures were done, we walked for miles, from city to country and everything in between. Just recently our government has decreed that we fall back again. That means that the end of our walk, our day and our daylight arrive a bit earlier.

One Autumn evening, in an up-east residential area where our walking-tour had come to an end, I found myself outside an apartment building in a modest neighborhood. Standing in the shadows between daylight and darkness, I was able to catch a glimpse of America, as a peeping Thomas Jefferson. That glimpse coincided with the evening news and each window cast the glow, flicker and politics, of the television channel chosen by its owner. For all the years of my growing up, I knew our family T.V. was where we would find the latest news and information. But this evening as I watched, I realized that I could hear the voices of the commentators, one railing against the other. They were doing their best to incite hatred for anyone who failed to toe-the-mark and believe whatever "they" were espousing .

Where was it that we lost our respect for one another? At what point did we throw out the "civil" baby with the "disrespectful" bathwater?

Oh, how I love my nation and how dearly I love my neighbors... That has nothing whatsoever to do with the "Vote for My Candidate," sign in their front yards. If we require agreement on everything before we can love, we have lost all hope.

Love comes first and all else follows!

Tigger indeed loves you...

Coyote

It's the first day of winter on the top of Doug's Mountain; sunrise of the longest night and the birth of the shortest day of the year. The air is cold, the sky is dark blue and the last of the twinkling stars are winking *adios*. Tis a lucky morning for me, there is not a breath of desert wind. My good fortune, because the animals that I love so dearly cannot smell or sense my presence.

Looking out across the silent Las Vegas valley, to the dawn-brushed snowcapped mountains, I am mid prayer, when a tawny flash catches my photographers' eye. Below me and crossing the desert from right to left, is a beautiful coyote. Picking his way in and out of the sage brush, yucca, juniper and creosote, he appears to be heading home from a long night of hunting, to feed his family.

Coyotes mate for life and are excellent neighbors. We know exactly where this fine fellow has his den. Beneath the earth his family sleeps, awaiting his return. His range is about two square miles and his diet consists of rodents, fruit, vegetables, and any small critter who wanders our streets and trails unsupervised. We own a famous cat-author, but we have no worries for her safety. "Three O'clock On The Nose" is an indoor cat!

As the first brush of dawn fills our valley, I can celebrate one of my favorite morning shows: sunrise on the houses below, the ones that shelter my neighbors and friends.

As the new year shakes off its repose, wipes the sleep out of its eyes and comes awake, we await the first serenade of our coyote sisters and brothers. It will be a sign that life is as it should be, and we are where we should be in this wonderful universe...

Thank you...
Tigger

Wings

Ever since I was a small cowboy, I have always been fascinated and moved by the sound of wings... Whether feathered or spiritual, beneath the stars above my campsite or off across the mighty ocean, the presence of wings has lifted me up and transformed my life and my being.

The first time I was introduced to the power of wings in my life, I was sitting uncomfortably in a chapel, listening to some very boring music presented by a group of choir boys, which included my older brother. It was Christmastime and I wanted to be out in the woods or up on my horse, exploring. At least outdoors I could be looking for Santa Claus. As my eyes wandered around the room, wishing I could escape or at least catch a glimpse of nature through the stained-glass windows, I heard faintly, the lyrics of the carol being sung. *"Angels We Have Heard on High..."* I wondered, had anyone ever really heard angels singing. *"And the mountains in reply..."* How dearly I loved the *"sunlight and shadows"* of the mountains. If only I could get outside. *"Joy to the World." "Hark the Herald angels sing."*

Although I was unaware at the time, I was being sweetly seduced by the glory and passion of the hymns of the holidays. One by one I began to hear the words, *"Go Tell It on the Mountain," "Oh Holy Night,"* and then with the soft young voices inviting me to *"Sleep in heavenly peace,"* I began to feel the meaning and the calling of the lyrics and the spirit of this music. It was the birth of my joy for Christmas music.

Today it is my honor to sing, recite and perform this holy music, from our dining table to churches and auditoriums. Only now this little cowboy sings with the brush of blessed wings on my heart.

Amen...
Tigger

"Cool"

I love this long-outdated expression: "C-O-O-L!" Throughout the decades, these four simple letters have been used to describe a good situation, a great outfit, a certain style of west coast jazz, *"The Cool School,"* a line from the title of a Little River Band song, *"Cool Change,"* a movie star in favor for the moment and more importantly a desired physical condition on a scorching hot desert day.

I am always honored to speak in schools. I am invited to teach and inspire but whatever the grade level, I go to learn. The language of the young is a treasure chest of *"What's happening now,"* as my friend Flip Wilson called it, Awks (awkward), Cancel (reject), Cheddar (money), and of course Sic, the latest version of "Cool..." We were Sic once, not so long ago and we were sure that we were cool.

I also enjoy and celebrate the language of the animals. All the creatures on earth and as we may soon learn, throughout the universe, require a certain reasonable temperature to live, function and thrive on the face of this wonderful water-planet. With the onslaught of our summer temperatures in the southwestern desert, we wonder...How do all these living things remain cool?

Question: *If I lick my arms to remain cool, what kind of creature am I? If I build my nest to include air conditioning, what kind of insect am I? If I use my wings to keep myself and my colleagues from overheating, who am I? If I flap my gullet to maintain my temperature, who am I? If I use my tail to create shade from the summer sun, who am I?*

Cool! That's what they are. Kangaroos, termites, bees, pelicans, and ground squirrels are just a few of the life forms that use special adaptations to maintain a healthy temperature in the heat of summer. No sweat or YOLO (you only live once)!

Turn up the air, please!
Tigger

The Flame

Within each of us there burns a flame of life. As long as this flame burns we remain alive. Once it is extinguished, life exits our body and we are no longer of this earth. How we care for and about this flame, during our time here, is of great importance. We have every right to fall asleep in peace each evening and to awaken each morning in joy. The power to arouse this gift, is in our hands and of our making.

No one can deliver peace of mind to us. It cannot be purchased online or found in any store. It happens when we breathe, in such a way that our hearts and lungs dance with the universe. It happens when we choose our diet from those things that feed our fire. It happens when we find, in the midst of each busy day, a moment in which we allow the flame to rest, as if it were in a windless place. Do not stress and fret about how and when to do this…Simply begin to think about what we have shared and allow it to happen.

Some years ago my audiences began to ask about my journey. They came to learn about the nuts and bolts of my system for life and business but eventually they began to ask if I would consider creating and presenting a seminar about the pathway. Thanks to those adventuresome folks, the "Spritsong Retreats," were born.

Imagine carrying your folding chair, pillow, blanket and water jug into the wilderness for an inspirational program. The Bob Marshall Campground, South Dakota, Grand Mesa, Colorado, Peoa Valley, Utah, and the Strawberry Lodge on the creek in Kyburz, California, where we shared the space that once served as an 1858 stage coach stop. These were a handful of places that called us to share the flame.

From the song that I composed as a theme for the Spritsong retreats: *"Listen to the water. Can you hear the wind? Listen to the earth and to each other and now the song begins... Spiritsong."*

Keep your prayers, keep the flame,
Tigger

Kindness

I have the hardest time watching the news on television. They start in the morning with bombshell breaking news and then continue to repeat the same drear and horrifying stories over and over again. Enough!

I must say that I understand why David Muir and his "ABC World News Tonight" broadcast, is so highly rated and popular. At least he and his producers forsake the doom and gloom, to end each broadcast on a hopeful note.

My readers know that I am a fan of great medicine and a supporter of fine physicians. Perhaps you will understand, when I say that for the last ten years, we have searched for a family doctor, in whom we could put our trust and confidence. Oh, we have had our annual exams and been faithful to our necessary labs and visits, but we never felt the connection we do with our other trusted medical providers.

At last we hit the jackpot in the person of Dr. Panesar! She is young, extremely well qualified, highly recommended and a joy to know. During our initial visit Dr. "Pan" revealed to us that she was married to a physician of great stature. His name was Dr. Tsui...

So tonight, when David Muir teased his usual positive closing segment, revealing that something special had happened at the Spring Valley Hospital in Las Vegas Nevada, naturally I stayed tuned for my hometown story.

Back from the commercial, we saw a piece of video featuring an exhausted housekeeper, in her scrubs, watching, as a doctor in full-on hazmat gear, was giving her a break by cleaning and sterilizing the room for her. An incredible gift of kindness in a very stressed and weary world. The Housekeeper, Irene Abar, almost in tears of thanks, was recognizing Dr. Kevin Tsui, M.D. for his kindness and support.

Dr. Tsui, is the husband of our wonderful new friend and physician, Dr. Pan... Small world with some wonderful people in it.

A thankful Tigger

The Bowl

It is one-thousand steps up from the valley floor to, "the bowl." On a cold desert morning, there is nothing like sliding my hand onto the warm part of the twelve-million-year-old stone. Worn smooth by wind and weather, the dark boulder collects the sunlight and holds on, until lizards, snakes and hikers like myself, stop off to take advantage of nature's hand warmer.

What would you say if I told you I have climbed my beloved mountain in a rainstorm, only to be surprised by something special in the bowl...? As I ascended the steep slope toward the two-ton chunk of lava, I heard or thought that I heard tiny voices. Now, I have a wonderful imagination and so I shook my head and lifted the brim of my hat, to try to catch a glimpse of what I was hearing. The closer I came, the more I realized that my ears were not deceiving me... I was hearing not only laughter but splashing sounds as well. It was as if children, the smallest ever, were playing in mother nature's pool.

For my children and grandchildren, I have written and told many stories about gnomes and fairies but although I believe in little people, I have never crafted a report on my observations of these mysterious tiny creatures in the woodlands. Today I am taking a chance on you.

Starting a walk before dawn and remaining on the trail till after sundown, can reveal some wondrous sights. May I suggest a caution: This is a tale only for the young and young at heart. Most grownups have long since lost their willingness and therefore their ability to see and experience such wonders.

One day I will see you on the mountain and perhaps if we are quiet and of an open mind, we shall share some magic...

Tigger

Up!

Recently, our friend Ann Mincey, mentioned a favorite song, "You Raise Me Up," by Josh Groban. Goose pimples for me! That choice by my inspiring friend Annie Panda, got me thinking about the power and joy in the word, *Up*.

Jerry Seinfeld does a wonderful comedy routine about that word. After revealing that everything in the mind of parents is "down." *"Sit down, calm down, slow down and put that down."* He shares how everything to kids, is up... *"Wait up, hold up, shut up, what's up and why can't we stay up!"*

Our friend, the sweet voiced Nevada Hall of Fame Dee-Jay, Ted Quillin said, *"I may give out, but I'll never give up!"*

I loved the film *Up*. The idea of tying thousands of balloons to your house, to fly away and fulfill a lifelong dream, lifts me up indeed. The love story of the animated stars, Carl and Ellie, would touch the hearts of even the coolest character and the fact that the two young explorers wrote their dreams down on paper and then kept a diary faithfully over the years, suits me fine.

The fact that the loyal dog who befriended them, was named Dug, was alright with me too... *"Squirrel!"*

If you have never seen this film, give yourself a gift and do so. If you have had the pleasure, go back over what you saw and more importantly remember the wonderful voice-overs you recall. To live long and well, we truly need to be animated. *Up* is just that, a chance to get up and get moving whether we walk or roll along we need to move our body, mind, and spirit. I have heard people say that they don't know how to dance. You have been dancing since you were conceived. Don't stop now!

Will you stand UP with me?
Tigger

Heart Work

Have you ever helped complete a one-thousand piece-jigsaw puzzle? What was the artwork that attracted you? Sunrise on The Beach, Harry Potter, Doughnuts, Cats or Dogs? There is something very wonderful about joining family and friends around the table on a snowy fireplace evening. It was a deep winter night and we were on Lake Winnipesaukee, in New Hampshire trying to re-create the artwork we first saw on the cover of the box. Now imagine doing the same thing with a million tiny pieces of colored sand.

A mandala is a geometric configuration of symbols, with a very unusual purpose. This beautiful piece of art is a sacred vision and to some, it represents the cosmos metaphysically or symbolically. It is used as an aid to focus. Beginning with one tiny grain of sand, these entrancing pieces of heart-work, pour forth from the hands and spirit of only the most patient monks.

Built with incredible care and devotion, as a form of meditation, these bright, intricate geometric designs are a reflection and revelation of their Buddhist teachings. Herein, you may find the earth, the heavens, and the universe itself.

Devoting hours and sometimes days to the gathering of this coarse sand and mixing the pigments, it is all about the process, not the product. The artwork, the monks say, transmit positive energy to the environment and to those who are fortunate enough to view them.

However long the creation takes, from hours to days, it will be prayed over and then, to the dismay of the uninitiated, the monks will destroy this cosmic diagram, sending it back into the universe from whence it came. In the words of my friend George Harrison, *"All Things Must Pass!"*

As back into the box, we return the thousands of colorful pieces, we are reminded that we are those pieces, those wonderful, unique shapes, and colors. We know that our world will never quite be whole until we find that perfect-fit place of our belonging.

Peace and Blessings,
Tigger

The Young Professors

How can I thank thee, let me count the ways? Do you have kids? We either have them or we once were them. That's just how it works. When our first to be born was on the way, I was scared to death. I was sure I had no idea what to do with that marvelous lump of life. Our dad, "Charlie Brown" as I nicknamed him, really helped when he looked me square in the eye and said, *"Don't worry Dougbert, children grow up in spite of their parents."* He was right.

As to how one becomes a father, that is a different story. I can tell you true, my kids played a major role in helping to raise me. Our first born, Linda, (Spanish for beautiful) is astounding. She became a world class Flamenco Dancer. Dubbed by her peers, "La Matadora," she not only dances and appears in films but is an instructor of the highest repute. Linda inspires me! Second to arrive was Barbee. From Barbara Jane, I learned the ways of a steady hand on the tiller. She navigated twenty-one years on this planet before she was killed in a single car crash, in the California desert. Barbee still inspires me! Steven D. arrived to help me understand that all children are born with backpacks and when they get good and damn ready to leave, they will. So happy to have him back. Steve is on the tracks of his dream, as he manages a great restaurant here in Boulder City, Nevada. Steve inspires me!

The next three wonders adopted me and have added so much to our whole family. California Chris is a master fine wood worker, who helped to construct George Lucas' recording studio on the ranch. C.A. Inspires me! Dave (The Mighty One) is a retired elevator man, an exceptional father, grandfather, and son. He has taught me the most about being a dad. I pity the trout that finds my son in his or her stream. *"Fish On!"* Dave Inspires me! Colorado Chris is the youngest of our brood. An accomplished artist and illustrator, he is also a master hair stylist and colorist. From him I have come to understand that the differences between us are not only right but worth celebrating. Christo is a deep and wise thinker. C.B. Inspires me!

Since these treasures began arriving and setting examples for their dad, Doug Cox is becoming a much better man. I love you all beyond measure.

Tigger

Meow!

What is the most popular pet chosen by owners here in these United States? If you are anything like me, your mind races in the hope that the answer returns in your favor. Let's see...

Cat people are weird and wonderful! I know because I are one... We just made our annual visit to the Las Vegas Cat Show. What a "mind movie" it was. The cats, oh-my-the-cats, but the owners as well, were worth the price of admission. They have a certain style and look that simply defies description.

I for one, just out of the celebration of life, for the passing of a dear friend, wore a sport jacket and a tie. (I was the only one.) The others, unlike their prized felines, ranged from movie star finery, to a number of other outfits that would make any Walmart shopper proud.

The feline beauties that lounged or played in their carry-cages, were magnificent. Whatever your taste in furry friends, you could find it at the show. Although many of the breeders were offering their cats and future kittens for sale, you could hardly tell it from their demeanor. They ranged from sullen to surly, with an occasional smile and an offer to show and discuss the possibilities of purchase, for up to $1000.

I truly enjoy walking and re-walking the show floor, examining the wonderful creatures, and learning from the talented judges, as they put the hopefuls through their paces and eventually selected the top three. Tough job!

For me, the highlight of this year's event, as I walked among the cages, was the moment when I commented on a beautiful Bengal Cat. *"You are so beautiful,"* I said. The owner, without looking up replied, *"Thank you darling..."*

By the way: #1 Fish, #2 Cats, #3 Dogs

Tigger loves cats and dogs! =^..^=

Misty!

Our world has changed much since I arrived into it many years ago. Although each generation has its wonders and challenges, I am convinced that having family generations share the same house, is a lifelong treasure. Our maternal grandma and grandpa came to live with us when we were very young, and they were quite elderly. Among the myriad of gifts bequeathed to me, grandpa taught me how to prepare and bake the most scrumptious cobbler with peaches fresh off our tree and grandma, bless her soul, taught me how to read when I was just three years old. That revelation opened a doorway into a treasure trove of adventures and a window onto a world of imagination. Reading, and being read to, allowed me to go anywhere and any when and I did just that.

I love horses and I've always been enchanted by the ocean. What a perfect setup! Little wonder then, that on my tenth Christmas, my grandmother, who knew me so well, presented me with a special Gift. It was a brand-new book, titled *Misty of Chincoteague*, written by Marguerite Henry, and illustrated by Wesley Dennis.

This beautiful book introduced me to the wild horses who make their home on the beaches of Virginia and to a family who raised a wild filly they named Misty. I write this now because I am always reminded of these wild and wonderful ponies, whenever a hurricane threatens the Atlantic coastline.

As a young lad, I worried about the fate of these powerful equine creatures, running wild in the face of a monster storm. I know now of the natural survival instincts of these beauties and how, since the sixteen- hundreds, they have successfully weathered many such cyclones.

If you recently found yourself immersed in the weather channel, turn it off, put on some soft music and download this wonderful book. It is a window on a world, that most of us will never experience.

See you on Chincoteague in the spring...
Tigger

Mosskins!

The beautiful John Portman-designed Hyatt Hotel, in downtown Atlanta is a classy place to stay. We were in town preparing to present a seminar for the wonderful folks of Georgia. In the middle of our Saturday setup and rehearsal, one of our team-members piped up and asked, *"Hey! Who wants to go for a swim in the lake?"* In unison we all replied, *"Yes indeed!"*

Turns out, she had an uncle who kept a boat on lake Allatoona. In twenty minutes, we were in the car and on our way. The lake is less than an hour from the hotel and as we drove, I suggested that we make a day of it and go water skiing while we were there. We pulled off and headed for the first hardware store we could find, to buy a ski. The clerk let on that he had never sold just one ski, so we took a pair and he threw in a piece of rope for $49.95. Look out lake... Here we come.

Once at the lake, it was decided that I should go first, since it was my idea and so I dropped off the back of Uncle Jack's boat, let the rope run tight and yelled, *"Hit It!"* It was a strange sort of a houseboat ski, but I was up and, on my way, first try. I cruised along on top of that warm southern water, until I thought that someone else deserved a turn. I signaled for the dismount and skied up onto the beach.

Uncle jack pulled his boat up and commented that it was a dang good thing I was a such good skier. My question, *"Why?"* His answer, *"That lake is just filled with Mosskins!"* Our country host was referring to the fact that the lake was loaded with Water Moccasins and they can be a bit aggressive and very poisonous. I made it back unbitten and it was great to be onstage in front of our "Gone with The Wind" audience...

Tigger

History and Magic

The fireplace was crackling just behind me; the flames danced and filled our cozy living room with light. The future seemed to lie just ahead and with our youngest heading into his teen years, time was running out.

Where does one find magic? In a cynical and distrustful world, I often turn to youth and such it was on that cold November afternoon, high in the Rocky Mountains. This was the last evening of daylight-saving time and I wasn't about to let that one precious hour slip away.

A sweet, fragrant rain had passed through earlier and the hint of snow was in the air, when I extended the invitation. *"Let's head up to the top of the mountain, create some magic and make it home in time for supper... What do you say?"* We were always creating adventures on the spur of the moment and so my twelve-year-old's nod, was all it took. I had a plan in mind as we crossed the moist ranch road and headed straight up for the ridge at the top of Sweetwater Canyon.

At the crest, my son looked at me to see what I had cooking in my storytellers' mind. Campfires were a part of everything we did, whether in the mountains or on the beach. They were a part of our food prep and survival. Once on top, our son instinctively began to clear a fire spot. Whether or not the fire was ever lit, the assumption that it was safe dry and ready was a part of our discipline.

We indeed lit the fire and let it settle into beautiful dark ash before I said, *"Let's write a charcoal message and hide it on the underneath side of these rocks..."* And that is what we did.

So somewhere on the Sweetwater Lake Road, just above 8236 feet there is a message from son to father and father to son on twelve-million-year-old rocks.

Heading up to see if we can find them one day soon...
Tigger

My Desk

Memories! I hope that your family shares a-plenty... It seems that in this life we do collect a bunch of stuff. The best "things" are the objects that carry us back to the treasured moments of days gone by. It seems that for me these things end up by design or by magic, on my desk or in my office.

The beautiful autographed Hard Rock guitars, and the service awards from those who gave me the opportunity to serve are a part of the display. The gold records from the radio and music business that was so good to me, the bust of Abe Lincoln with his Santa hat, all remind me that it is people and pets who leave behind the best memories.

Our Cowboy Christmas tree which, every year, takes up residence in front of my desk, is covered with décor and artifacts reaching back a century or more. The walls around me are hung with artists names like Bama, Clymer, Kelly and Cox. My beautiful wood gun cabinet wherein resides my mother's Winchester twenty-two rifle, which was a gift to her from our dad, on her twenty-first birthday, are all a part of the wonder.

When next you sit down, at your desk, couch, or patio chair, to write a note, address a holiday message, look into your smart phone or send an email, take a good look around and "see" the treasures that give you comfort. It is these things that inspired Kenny Loggins to write, *"Please, celebrate me home..."*

So... what happens to all these "things" when it's time to change the guard? One of my sons suggested that my office be left intact and bequeathed to my offspring. I guess I'm not the only romantic in the group.

Je Me Souviens...
Tigger

Mystery

Just received an email from the great *Michigan Frank*. I had sent my friend the Facebook photo of Big Foot playing saxophone in the woods. It was titled "Saxsquatch!" Pretty funny eh? Frank responded that he was watching a TV show, in which they had the elusive creature, surrounded in the northwest woods of Washington.

Have you ever considered how devastating it will be, when these intrepid hunters actually do capture the "Squatch?" What will they do then? Where will they go? A life's work will have slipped through their fingers and it will all be over. A whole industry will disappear from our economy. So many copy-cat TV shows will go down the drain, leaving all of those producers and camera folks, out in the woods. It will be the end of an era, except of course for the museum.

One would think that the resting place of that beast, would be in the northwest, where the fearless loonies had spent so much time tracking him (or her). It turns out that the crusty old leader of the group, prefers not to retire in rainy old Washington and instead will head for the sunshine of Wickenburg, AZ. His roadside stand and museum will reside in the back corner of that gas station. Right on highway 93, just past the Mike O'Callaghan-Pat Tilman Memorial Bridge, we will find, for sale, plaster casts of giant footprints, bits of hair and CD's of the blood curdling scream, of the beast that built an industry. An unusual C.E.O., don't you think?

I never want to know how the magician does the illusion. I never want to lose my sense of wonder. I hope they never catch that handsome, hairy rascal. I love a mystery, don't you?

Tigger is not afraid... He can out-bounce a yeti, anyway!

New Growth

Have you ever observed that people in the supermarket or hardware store often stop to look at babies and young children? They don't spend a lot of time on geezers like me or middle agers like you, but they fawn over the newbies. For me, the same is true of days and seasons.

It is early summer in the beautiful Rocky Mountains and as my eyes trace the morning skyline before me, every growing thing seems to be putting on a show. *"Look at me, look at me,"* they seem to be saying. Flora and fauna are begging for my attention and everywhere I look, I see new life and fresh birth.

My favorites must be the beautiful Blue Spruce trees because they leave nothing to our imagination. How these beautiful conifers have wintered, is obvious. Beneath their outerwear, the color of last year's needles is there to help us remember but the bright green expose of the year's new growth, is unmistakable. In the toughest winters, the contrast can be sparse but in good years, as this has been, it is a beautiful new Red-Carpet ready, outfit.

When thinking of living creatures, I always recall Jim Herriot's wonderful book, *All Things Great and Small.* and ask myself about my new growth? How have I evolved physically, financially, emotionally and spiritually during the last year. Would I have fresh new stories to share and new wisdom to reveal?

I am one of those, who always tries to look for the best in things and people. I really enjoy sharing genuine compliments and new growth is the birthplace of the best of those. Today I am looking over my own inventory of thoughts and actions, to make sure that I am not stuck and repetitious but, on the way, *"Up and out,"* as Roald Dahl had Willy Wonka put it.

Working on being a better Tigger

The Night Sky

These July days feel like the inside of a baker's oven. The sun burns down on the barren sand, like a welding torch and our beloved *Desert Wind,* sweeps across the thirsty saguaros. It is a blow drier for giants. Even the rattlesnakes slither for shelter from the dangerous solar radiation. This is summer in the American southwest.

I love it here. This is not a landscape for sissies. Just as surely as the day arrives, with the rising sun, over the rim of Doug's Mountain, the blessed darkness of evening follows. It pulls up the shade of a new time, a new temperature and a whole new view of the universe.

Step outside our home, walk straight into the wild and look up. Allow your eyes to rest and adjust. In a matter of moments, your light abused vision will begin to perceive the spiritual revelations of the velvet night sky. Like magic, the universe will begin to reveal itself to you.

The big dipper, the southern cross and Orion's belt, are so close, it seems they are there for the touching. At the end of the little dipper handle, forever pointing the way north, shines Polaris or as the Polynesians call it, *"The star that is always there."*

I particularly enjoy bringing my I-Pad out into a light free place and clicking on my *"Skyview,"* app. There before me is a planetarium's display of the night sky. Common planets and constellations appear for my enjoyment. On into the tiniest pin pricks of light, I am informed and enlightened. I wonder, am I perhaps looking into the future home site of humankind?

It is and always will be there, for those of us who have eyes and a child's sense of wonder. Somewhere out there, I'll be waiting!

Tigger

Pirates

The tropical breeze was warm and fresh... We had just sailed in, bare sticks, from Jost Van Dyke. Along the way we had passed Great Thatch, Frenchman's Cay, Dead Chest, Pelican and Ginger Island. Between Spring and Devils Bay we put into The Baths, one of the eight natural wonders of the Caribbean.

In three fathoms of crystal blue water, we dropped the hook over the bow, dove into the eighty-degree water and swam for shore. I made note of the fact that it was a fifty-yard swim, remembering that after a day ashore, we would need to return to our sailboat.

As I thought about the names of the romantic places we had passed on our journey, my imagination turned to pirates. There is a marvelous history of these bloodthirsty rascals throughout the Caribbean and so it was, that I swam ashore with a patch over one eye, a cutlass in my belt and a treasure map tucked into the pouch in my britches.

In this wonderful water world, there are huge boulders and caves to explore. Lighted from above by a brilliant tropical sun, the reflection off the water onto the cave walls, danced and played with us for a magical three hours.

On the return to the boat, I was pleased with myself, that I had saved enough energy to make the swim safely. We were, in the afternoon, swimming against the wind and we used every bit of strength we had, to make it safely back onboard. The rum-in-pineapple was sweet and welcome that evening, as we hoisted the anchor and headed for our next adventure.

There were four of us buccaneers on that voyage and I am touched to say that one of us has sailed on. *"Tell me Jim, do you think we'll ever go treasure hunting again?"* (Captain Long John Silver) The second star to the right and straight on till morning. Oh, lucky you, Peter, and the Boys.

Tiggarrrrrgh!

Prestidigitator

In the huge ballroom of the Airport Hilton Hotel, the audience sat in anticipation. As the hour of the program drew near, twenty-five-hundred world class hair artisans and business leaders from around the world, awaited. The house lights dimmed and the room fell silent, we were ready to present our surprise.

What was about to be revealed upon that stage, had been in serious and rigorous rehearsal for weeks. The theme was Camelot and our leaders John and Paula, were to portray King Arthur and his Queen. Magic was the theme for our presentation and three of us were invited to share an illusion with our wonderful guests.

My effect, or "trompe l'oeil," was to bring forth fire from my empty hands and I must say that it took every day from my initiation to that moment onstage to get it right. We were trained by top magicians from the Magic Castle and the audience was indeed astounded. During my presentation from the main stage, I brought forth before my mountain man's blanket/robe, my empty hands, out of which, in the darkened room, I produced a bright burst real fire.

At the company party following the show, I (as Merlin) was invited and honored to sit at the raised head table beside Queen Guinevere, where her guests passed in review. What fun it was to invite the queen's subjects to choose one of three empty wine glasses on the table, out of which I would then produce fire. At the conclusion of our most successful event, I met with the magician who had been my coach and trainer. I was honored that he thought my illusion had been presented exceptionally well and he asked, *"Would you like to know how some other tricks are executed?"* My answer was, *"No!"* I never want to lose my sense of wonder.

Tigger

Rest

Are you a good sleeper? I am... Perhaps a better question might be, are you a good *rester*? During my presentations around the world, I often ask my audiences, whatever their ages, this exact question, *"Do you rest well at night?"* From kids to seniors, the answer is, *"No!"* I ask, because I have discovered and am convinced that a good night's rest is the best doctor in the world. When we are truly resting, we are healing mind, body and spirit!

For me, the act and art of resting well, begins long before my head hits the pillow. Nothing shatters the joy of bedtime like the flashing, shrieking glass box, that sits before you, in your TV room. Turn it off at least thirty minutes prior to head on the pillow time. Begin your sweet deep breathing at the same time and then bring that precious life sustaining oxygen with you, when you come to bed. On first recline, lie on your back with your face toward the sky and allow your body to sink joyfully into your mattress. Now breathe in the wonder of those things you most hold dear. In whatever manner you pray, give thanks for all that is good and right with your life and times. Now rest!

One day, in the midst of some very high-level executive meetings upstairs in the Hard Rock, I took advantage of a break, to head for the restroom. In the boardroom next to us, was a group of strangers, hard at work on something that had obviously taken away their smiles. Spying one member of their team seated alone, I scooted in the door and said howdy, welcome to Seminole Gaming. I Handed him my card and he returned the favor with his own information. Once back in our meeting, I took the liberty of sending an email to my new friend and I jokingly said I hoped that he and his colleagues might find the smiles they were looking for. He immediately responded with a series of smiley emoticons and I made a lifelong friend of Rest West!

And that is his real name!

Aloha Tigger (zzzzzzzzzzzzzzzz)

Reverence Lost

Where are they now, the ones we once looked up to, coach, friend, minister, rabbi, scout master, grandparent, or teacher?

Lost in our electronic devices, we no longer share or receive the feeling of deep respect. Our world seems to have lost the sense of awe, esteem, and appreciation, that once gave a richness to our days and nights. In too many families, parents and elders are no longer cherished, honored, and revered!

I learned about the depth and wonder of this blessed worship, when I first read *The Wind in the Willows,* the children's book, by Kenneth Gahame. In the brilliant morning light, the water rat, and his friend the mole are searching for a lost little otter, when they come face to face with the great "Friend and Helper." *"Then the two animals, crouching to the earth, bowed their heads and did worship."* I know that feeling and I love that place.

I never wish to live a day without moments of reverence. My heart and soul are so filled with gratitude for family, friends, and memories. My anticipation of the days ahead and my celebration of this world around me, are inspiration enough, to bring tears of joy and a prayer of thanks.

As a young Scout Master, I worked so hard to earn the trust of the boys who joined our troop and garner the respect of the parents who had placed their young men in my care. I wanted very much to be a good guide but more than that I wanted to be a model of behavior for these fine young men. Today I see too many adults expecting obedience from young people who have never been shown the way. We all need to be inspired to do the right thing.

At a time when the words and voices of our leaders no longer hold us spell-bound, may we each find a quiet, holy place, in which to offer a sincere and reverent thanks, for the wonder that surrounds us.

Amen...
Tigger

Sage

I have so many wonderful friends in Texas. Truth be told, I have always loved Texas. In fact, when I was a kid, our family used to sing dinner-table songs about Texas, *"The Stars at Night are Big and Bright, (clap-clap-clap-clap) Deep in the heart of Texas."* I'll bet you did too.

The joy of this memory goes even deeper. Growing wild and wonderful on the 350 acres around our southern California home, the woods and fields were covered in sage brush! *"The sage in bloom is like perfume, (clap-clap-clap-clap) Deep in the heart of Texas."* The fragrance of the sage in Eaton Canyon, that rubbed off on my Levi's, boots, and shirts, inspired me to think... Why couldn't I create a sage perfume as a gift for my mom?

I collected a handful of the beautiful pale green leaves of the ubiquitous sage plant and immersed them in alcohol. I knew that the famous perfumes my glamorous mom wore, all contained alcohol. That was my formula. In a mason jar, borrowed from our pantry, I placed the sage leaves in the alcohol, hid it in my closet and then waited.

Anticipation is a fine wine. Once we put a plan in motion it gets pretty itchy under the saddle blanket until the process is complete and that cover is pulled off to reveal the hidden treasure.

When an appropriate amount of time had passed, with great enthusiasm, I brought forth the magic perfume and presented it to the woman who had given me life. When I shared my horrifying elixir, she was as wonderful and kind about it, as always. *"Oh, thank you Dougbert..."* She would say and I knew that I had done it again, for the first time in a row. As a child, did you ever create a handmade gift or treasure that you knew was the gift of a lifetime? Me three...

Tigger

Say Yes!

How many times have you said, *"It's too cold!" "It's too windy!" "It's raining!" "It's too far, too dusty,"* or a million other excuses... Well... now it is too late! As you are reading this book, the old wooden gates at Bonnie Springs Ranch have closed for the last time. The place where these stories were born, has been sold and the ranch is closing forever.

For more than thirty years we have been visiting "The Ranch," rain or shine. From the wild burros on the dusty mile long roadway, to the old western town, we have loved every minute of it. On many a cold, windy, desert morning, we have pushed our way through the swinging doors and into the historical restaurant, to sit by the woodfire and share hot coffee and a true ranch breakfast. We have said *"Yes,"* many times each year.

Sitting on the fence at the stables, with the smell of hay and horses, listening to the creaking of old saddles and the call of mourning doves, Bonnie Springs has been our gateway to the honest-to-goodness old west. Under the crystal-clear night sky, we have listened to the coyotes singing to a billion stars. How fortunate we are, that our family and friends never said, *"No"* when the invitation came.

My friends, family, and faithful readers, wherever you live, there is a Bonnie Springs, park, zoo, museum, hiking trail or equestrian center, quite near you... The next time you are fortunate enough to be invited, go, grab the chance, capture the moment, and say *"Yes!"*

To our great joy, Bonnie's neighbor, The Spring Mountain Ranch, is open and awaits our arrival even today. Perhaps the needlepoint tribute that hangs in the historic old Ranch house today, says it best: *"I will always feel the whisper of the desert wind, smell the sage, and see the stars above the mountaintops."* Buster Wilson 1908-1972 (One of the owners)

I will see you out there...
Tigger

Desert Shrimp

It's scorpion season in the desert. They appear in the yard, around garages and in our swimming pools. Desert Shrimp, as I call them, do have a venomous sting but they eat insects, carry their one hundred plus young on their backs and dance in the moonlight; that works for me.

Did you know that all scorpions fluoresce under ultraviolet light, such as an electric black light or natural moonlight? Scientists believe that this fluorescence may protect scorpions from sunlight, help them find each other or it might serve to confuse their prey. Perhaps that is why these nocturnal creatures are less active on moonlit nights and during the full moon.

In the four seasons of the television series, *Scorpion*, Elyes Gabel and Katherine McPhee played the almost romantic leads in this dramatic program. I don't know what the ratings were for the show because I had no interest in who else was watching. I simply had fun, sitting with my wife, and enjoying a professionally written, well-acted, adventure. I also enjoyed knowing that as we watched this story about geniuses and prodigies, we ourselves had that same genius within us. We don't know everything that others know but we sure know things that others do not.

In 25 years, you have lived through about 9,000 days. In 50

years, you have experienced 18,000 days. Every day and every moment of your life, the circuits of your mind have been gathering information. That is why I love to sit and talk with you. As Tommy Lee Jones said, to Will Smith, in *Men in Black*, *"Imagine what you will know tomorrow!"*

Talk to me,
Tigger

Seabird

For a seven-year-old child, life in the foothills outside of Pasadena, California was magical. Our large single-story farmhouse sat on seven acres of tree covered land. With a war going on, we provided as much of our own food as possible. I must have been a particularly good and trustworthy lad, for I was allowed to wander freely around the thirty plus acres of our neighborhood.

We were blessed to have an author as one of our neighbors and I, by invitation, was on my way to meet Mr. Holling. For this little cowboy, it was a long (3/4 of a mile walk) to my destination. The pathway to his home was shaded by sweet smelling sycamore trees and my imagination and anticipation filled in everything else. Mr. Holling greeted me at the door and offered me fresh lemonade. With glass in hand, we headed straight away for his study.

I remember now, the faint fragrance of sweet pipe smoke in the air, as we entered his writing space. I was enchanted. The author pulled up a stool and sat me at eye level, so that I might truly watch him at work. I realized I had come, expecting to watch him as he wrote. It never crossed my mind that I might observe a great artist creating the actual illustrations for this beautiful book.

Seabird is the story of a hand carved "scrimshaw" ivory gull, who is carried as a mascot across the great oceans of the world, by four generations of seafarers. Imagine how wide my eyes got, as I watched in wonder, as each beautiful page was decorated under the hand of Holling Clancy Holling.

It is said that children rarely have patience for adult things but I remember with great honor, the journeys I made and the number of days I spent, watching my new friend patiently create the Caldecott Award winning children's book. I still re-read Seabird each year, only now it is for my great grandchildren.

Tigger Ahoy...

Skies

Morgana King, (Carmela Corleone in The Godfather) sings: *"A time for summer skies, for hummingbirds and butterflies..."* This beautiful song, *"A Time for Love,"* composed by Johnny Mandel and Paul Francis Webster, is from the film, *"An American Dream."* What a magnificent world we live in. One in which the sky is always there above us, inviting us to imagine and envision. I am one of those who loves to watch the skies!

In our magnificent desert monastery, I can look up into a blazing blue summer sky and feel the searing sun and the hot sage kissed breeze across my face. On the beach, in Carmel, California, I can celebrate the fog, so cool and thick, that the droplets form a baptism across my brow. In the winter sky, above the fisherman's pier in Provincetown, Massachusetts, between the snowflakes, I spy *A Patch of Blue,* as the movie title proclaims.

In the charming animated film, *American Tail,* Fievel, the little mouse, separated from his family, sings about his hope to, *"Find one another."* You and I remember hearing Linda Ronstadt and James Ingram sing that touching song, *"Somewhere out there beneath the pale moonlight..."* The songs and movie titles are a wonder.

For me, the best memories of sky-gazing, are of lazy summer

afternoons on fresh cut grass, with my kids staring up into the tapestry above us, to find dragons, knights in armour and cartoon characters, scudding across the azure backdrop. *"Someone's thinking of me and loving me tonight!"*

Do you have a favorite memory song? A song that transports you somewhere and somewhen incredibly special, every time it plays? It is my hope that you have a dozen such treasured musical magic carpets that transport you instantly.

"Whatever skies above... I've known a time for spring, a time for fall but best of all, A time for love!"

Thank heavens!
Tigger

Hear Hear

Have you ever enjoyed watching the Macy's Thanksgiving Day Parade? In our home, it is a tradition to watch and listen, while we prepare our oh-so- thankful meal. This year I realized that the CBS broadcast booth was set in a way that our view of the hosts, also featured a wonderful memory. The New York Midtown Hilton Hotel was in the background of every shot. This year we spent a fabulous five days and nights, in that hotel with our friends from Intercoiffure. What a joy!

In big cities, there are so many things to experience. For me it's the sounds that come echoing up through the Canyons of glass and steel. During the day it is the grind of traffic and the pounding and clanging of the workers constant attempt, to repair the tired and pot-holed roadways of an ancient city. During the night while sound asleep and in dreamland, the cry of an emergency vehicle awakens me, as the uneasy sound of a siren dances up from the tired pavement. Hurrying to put out a fire, save a life or take a life; only tomorrow's newscast will reveal the rest of the story. We love New York.

During this visit we walked many miles from Strawberry Fields, past the ice rink in Rockefeller Center, to a fine lunch at the Hardrock in Times Square. The "big apple" has wonderful days but the nights on

Broadway are the magic...

Home now, at the monastery. It is five A.M in the cold darkness of a desert morning. Our house is still but for the purring of our cat on my desk and the sound of my fingers on the keys of my computer. The faint fragrance of a feast recently prepared, lingers in the air. As I sit anticipating the wail of a police car below, I am reminded where I am, by the solitary howl of a coyote. It is the southwest and that is one of the other sounds I love.

Tigger

Sentinel

I love meercats. What an intrigue it is, to sit quietly and observe the behavior of these precious little creatures. Whether it is critters in the zoo or folks in an airport, watching is the best sociology class on earth. On the top of a huge rock, in the Santa Barbara Zoo enclosure or on the highest branch of a Wait-a-bit Thorn bush, deep in the heart of the Kalahari Desert, a sentinel stands.

Closer to home, on the walls and cactus of our monastery, the familiar silhouette can be seen, keeping watch for the others of the flock. Whether meercat, gambel's quail, a mountain marmot, or a prairie dog on the great plains, some creature is always high up, alert and faithfully watching, searching, for approaching danger.

What a wonderful assignment. Such a high and worthwhile calling, for any creature to be so chosen. How joyful then, to be the human, selected to keep watch for our family, friends, neighbors, nation and at last, the earth.

The wonder of it all, is that in most cases, the sentinel is self-appointed. Some one of us simply makes the conscious choice, to keep watch over those we love. We forsake safety and ease, to climb to a position on high, where, wind, weather and predators be damned, we become lookout for those, other than ourselves.

All along the watchtower...

All of the fauna mentioned above, have a warning call to alert the colony to the danger. Prairie dogs, in particular, have a whole array of calls, to identify the specific predator on the move. Their language includes information about the type of interloper, speed, size, shape and color.

Have you ever assigned yourself or been assigned as a sentinel? As a father and scout master, I sure have. At the beach, lake or swimming pool, it is my honor and duty to stand guard and keep watch.

There is a "Sentinel Species," story in this book... Check it out.

To the future,
Tigger

A Moment

Gordon Lightfoot was performing at the Santa Monica Civic Auditorium. Backed up by his two regulars, Red Shea on guitar and John Stockfish on bass, Gord was holding us all in the palm of his hand. In the pencil spotlight shining down on the center of that magic stage, he sang, *"How long, said she, can a moment like this belong to someone?"* His voice was beautiful. It was one of the many times in my life, that a Gordon Lightfoot lyric set my mind to wondering. As Red and John surrounded Gordon with music, the packed audience surrounded the trio, with appreciation. We were given a voyeur's peak into an *Affair on Eighth Avenue*.

In my last book, *Mind Movies,* I included a scene about the importance of making our appreciation known to our friends and colleagues. I mentioned Gordon, because for my money, he is one of the greatest poets of our time and I was honored to be able to tell him so and often. Sad to realize that most of us never make the effort to share our appreciation, until it is too late. I have always felt that if someone offers a gift, we must make an effort to say thanks.

What does it take to say thank you to someone that we love... Thank you for clean sox and undies, a simple meal cooked and placed on the table, a freshly made bed or a glass of wine brought before the fire. It simply takes a moment.

My readers are so terrific about communicating with me. That is how I know you enjoy the invitations I insert into my stories. So here goes: Put on your Sennheiser Studio Headphones and cue up the *Canadian Railroad Trilogy*, the history of the building of the railroads across Canada. I am still astounded by the exquisite finger picking of the now departed Red Shea.

Do yourself a great favor and search out "If You Could Read My Mind," "Sundown," "Softly," or "Song for a Winters Night" and perhaps you will understand why Bob Dylan, listening to a Gordon Lightfoot song once said, he *"wished that it would last forever."*

What's the word? Some things that truly last forever only take a moment... *"Thank you, bless you, good job, well done, I'm so proud of you, I appreciate you!"*

Yep,
Tigger

The Jersey

Lucky man! In over one million plus miles of international travel, United Airlines only misplaced my bags once! It happened when I was on my way to a keynote presentation, in a huge ballroom at the Sheraton Universal Hotel, in North Hollywood. Flying in from Denver, I was dressed ready for roping. Without my gear, I immediately realized that this would not be the attire my host, Super Classy Redken Laboratories, would appreciate, so I began to formulate a plan.

Since my role onstage was that of life/business coach, I thought perhaps it would be acceptable to dress the part, so I asked my taxi driver to head for a sporting goods store. He did just that. Once inside, I began looking for a coach's windbreaker that would cover my "road-hard and put-up-wet look."

Nothing I found would suit the occasion. As I was just about to give up and exit the store, I spotted a football jersey. At that moment I didn't recognize the team colors, but I happened to like the number emblazoned on the front and back. It was 22! High energy in the universe my sister had shared with me. I only hoped it would turn out to be the highest energy number at the "Universal" hotel.

I stood in the darkness at the back of the huge ballroom, awaiting my introduction. The president made a few remarks and then said in a rather dry voice, *"Here is Doug Cox."* On pure adrenaline, I ran, full speed down the aisle, leaped onto the stage, turned directly to the audience of 1500 lecture weary folks, drank down a small bottle of one of the company's reconditioning products, tore my jacket open to reveal my football jersey and shouted, *"Good afternoon my friends!"* The place came unglued!

What good fortune. The shirt I had chosen turned out to be a Miami Dolphin game jersey. The year was 1972 and the team, under the direction of Head Coach Don Shula, became the only team to play an undefeated season. The audience loved my entrance with the cocktail and the reveal of the #22, to the point that for the next five years, that was my arrival onstage all over the world.

Rest in Peace Coach Shula... You are the Master.
Tigger

Sky Dance

It is a classic southwestern morning in early Spring. Illuminated by a brilliant sunrise, all of our senses are awakened for what is to come. Surrounded by the songs of our native birdlife and the fragrance of mesquite, creosote, pinion, juniper and sagebrush, the arms of our beloved saguaro are pointing the way, toward our day's adventure. We are headed up the mountain and away from people sounds and smells.

As the warmth begins to fill the desert morning, the sweet-scented air gathers along the base of the canyon walls and starts to rise and swirl, like a miniature tornado. Our star, like an Olympic Diver, pushes off the board and immediately is lifted with the rising warmth, to penetrate the sky.

At the cliff tops, she breaks the horizon and against the azure blue, her colors are magnificent. With wings like those of angels, she is striking, with a pale flecked underside, a darker belly band and cocoa colored back feathers. Her red tail is radiant against the sun and leaves no doubt about how she was named and who is the star of this film.

Riding the thermal, our magnificent raptor begins to call out in the familiar *"Screeeeeeeeech,"* that is so commonly heard in commercials and films. Whatever bird we may see on the screen, the sound that we hear, is most often a recording of the beautiful red-tailed hawk.

It is our lucky day, as I see above us, a solitary male, awaiting the arrival of his mate, for the ballet that will inspire a union, lasting a lifetime. Her large circles seem to trace those of her partner, until high above us, they become specks in our sky. Then suddenly, he turns over, into a death-defying dive and sweeps down toward the desert floor, finally turning up to return to his mate, their talons clenching, in a magic, mid-air adagio.

For one hour, we are treated to a sky dance, that will hopefully lead to the deposit of one to five eggs in their stick nest. Bless the papa hawk who will help to incubate these treasures and thereafter share in the feeding and rearing of the fluffy wonders. They will struggle through their shells, climb out into the light and within six weeks fly away.

A blessing,
Tigger

Fragrance

On the long, hot summer afternoons, we walk as always, only now, our pace is a bit slower. For a believer, there is the knowledge that just ahead, there is a treasure to be discovered. This new pace offers a time for practicing the gifts of our senses. To see, hear, touch, taste and smell the wonders of our world, is a such a blessing.

I see on the side of my pathway, a pair of mourning doves gathering stones to keep their digestive tract grinding away at the contents of their foraging. I hear the wings of honeybees, celebrating the presence of new pollen on the briefly blooming desert flowers. I love to touch the new growth of rosemary, as it rises up toward the light of the sun. Of all these joys, my greatest glory is and has always been, the fragrances that fill the one-hundred-degree air.

Whether it is a native plant, or a human introduced species, every breath is a wonder. Many of you know that my home was once Santa Barbara, California. That beautiful coastal city is a perfumed paradise. Out of all the tantalizing smells of that tropical place, I best remember Star Jasmine. The light, sweet aroma of this delicate white flower fills the night air and can carry me to a thousand places and remind me of a thousand romantic moments.

When we walk in our desert neighborhood, where High Mesa and Cypress Mesa meet, a special treat is waiting. As you approach from either direction, you can smell it... Santa Barbara! Our neighbors have planted a waterfall of this lovely plant, that cascades down from the treetop over the wall and beside the walkway. Every year it blooms, to carry us back to bike rides on the beach, walks through beautiful gardens and "Malulani," the scent of heaven.

Mother Nature is always sharing her story and her guidance. From the day we first catch a whiff of our star, the days of wine and jasmine are numbered. Too soon the white petals of our glory, will fall from the branches to cover the sidewalk and we will begin the patient anticipation of next year's arrival.

Unexpected pleasures are the greatest treasures!
Tigger

His Desk

Through a beautiful wrought-ironwork window-piece in his doorway, he sat typing away on his wonderful old manual *Royal* typewriter. Surrounded by his pride of polydactyl cats, comforted by his fine-china cup of English breakfast tea or an afternoon bracer of rum and tonic, I can only imagine what classics came to life, in this unassuming den. *The Sun Also Rises, The Snows of Kilimanjaro, A Farewell to Arms, The Old Man and the Sea,* these revered pieces of literature all came forth from a desk like this, in Ernest Hemingway's Home in Key West!

All of us write. From a love note in elementary school, to a novel that takes the literary world by storm, we are born authors. Do you have a desk, a place, an office, a secret spot where you go, when you are touched by your muse and want to put words to paper? If not, why not? Hiding in that infinite mind and spirit of yours, lurks a poem, a song, a love-note or a grand novel. Find your spot, take a seat and get started. Don't begin by worrying about the length or brevity. Don't be thwarted by how good or bad you think it might be; just get at it!

When I crafted my book, *Sh-Boom,* one of the things that moved me to design it as I did, was my desire to help people start writing and make it fun. I wanted them to play a part in setting forth their dreams. If you are going to write your life story, you sure ought to be holding the pen!

A simple but particularly important kick-off to writing, can be the act and art of journaling. It is a pleasure because you do not need to create the material you are writing; you simply need to set down a simple record of what happened today.

Remember to click "save" at the end, so you can whittle away at it in the days ahead. You are crafting your own private masterpiece... I know because that is how this book came to life.

We Write Together
Tigger

First Song

They say you never forget your first love. Perhaps, but I can assure you that I have never forgotten my first *song*. It was on a warm summer afternoon. The kind of day where you can smell everything that's been going on, up until that moment. Waffles, bacon, chicken, coffee, gardenias, and freshly cut lawns, all brought to us courtesy of a soft Santa Ana breeze. Perfect!

On our front porch, near the spot where the Rose Parade begins every New Year's Day, we sat together to share. Although they were here to take care of Little Dougie Cox, these were my friend's, and family. Salvador, and Rudy Osegera, were playing old Spanish guitars and Connie, their beautiful sister, was singing along. I was a mere two or three years old at the time, so guitars were a little big for me. I was holding mom's ukulele on my lap and trying to keep up.

The song was "Me Voy Pa'al Pueblo," and it began with some wonderful finger picking. I stared at Salvador's beautiful brown field-worn fingers on his ancient guitar strings and tried to copy what I was seeing and hearing. *Going to town,* is the story of a farm worker who has finished his labors for the day and is headed into town for some fun. He exclaims, *"I am going to cheer up my whole soul!"* I was trying so hard to make something of my little fingers on the uke, that Rudy, watching me very closely, decided to help me play the opening notes. He reached over and gently but surely placed my tiny fingers on the proper strings.

It took a few Saturdays but finally I got it. I could play along, and I began to sing. Perhaps it was fortunate that I had no interest in translating the beautiful words, en Espanol, so I never knew, until I was grown, that the farmer in the story also revealed that he was going to town because his wife didn't like parties or rum.

I still play and sing my first song, whenever I get the chance. I remember now fondly that we finished our day, en Pasadena, with their Madre, Senora, patting out and cooking tortillas on our grill for supper. Just one more wonderful fragrance to add to a marvelous day. Mi Vida es un milagro.

Gracias,
Tigger

Where or When

Our living room smelled wonderfully of popcorn, bourbon, and pipe tobacco. The carpet was rolled back and beautiful young people in uniforms, were dancing and holding on for dear life. It was early in 1942 and the air was filled with Glen Miller and laughter. I know now that we were laughing to keep from crying. I was five years old and oblivious to the gravity of the moments that surrounded us. It was not until one of those dancers did not return home from the war, that I became aware of the heartbreak of the conflict.

I may have been a kid, but I was very interested in the adults that came to visit and celebrate our fragile lives. On the piano bench, beside our friend Abel Decant, I found that many of these youthful revelers would come by to say *"Hi"* to Little Dougie Cox, Mrs. Cox's Kid. I loved it when Gray Ladies, in their nurse's outfits, and WAC's and WAVES, in their uniforms came over.

The hugs that accompanied their visits were surrounded in the fragrance of their perfume and gentle words.

During my lifetime, growing up and finding my way in the world of business, I have, as most of you know, chosen to become an inspirational speaker. I must truly confess that I was called to this adventure, rather than seeking it out. As both a teen and a young man, the last thing on my mind would have been to choose public speaking. I have been honored by the calling. My performances, throughout the world, have given me the gift of contact with thousands of people. Recently, I have been receiving communiques from many who recall "coming to see me!" I want to assure you that it was "I who came to see you!"

Raised during the war I came to realize, early on, how fragile life can be.

"We'll meet again, some sunny day..."
(Vera Lynn 1917-2020)

Tigger

Reminiscence of a Sweet Surprise (Part One)

Afternoons along the California coast are my favorites. The sun is low and golden through the moist air and the breeze smells like heaven. I hear the ocean calling me and I know it is time to go.

From my little home on Yankee Point Drive, in Carmel Highlands, the walk to the beach was a wonder. The morning glory blossoms, with their beautiful faces towards the sun and the Echium or Pride of Madeira, lined my way down the dirt path to the waterside. The glorious nasturtiums reminded me that a salad at suppertime would not be complete without a scattering of their blossoms.

Once on the beach the outgoing tide had left a collection of shells and other cast away treasures, that were not only a feast for the eyes but a bouquet for the nose. The only thing better than standing and observing, was to slip into the water quietly and smoothly, to lay back and float into my afternoon meditation. Crystal clear water below me and pale azure skies above. This was my holy place.

During meditation, time loses its place and meaning, so I didn't know how long I floated or what brought me out of my peaceful reverie, but I awakened to a sweet surprise. Lying beside me, wrapped in a golden swirl of kelp, was a baby otter. Wound carefully in the long strands, by his mother, he was sound asleep and a blessed companion. She had decided to head out to feed and did not want her little one to drift away during her absence.

Sea Otters are a glorious member of the marine life along the central California coast. Having once been hunted to near extinction and more recently threatened by a parasitic disease, they are treasures in the waters of the Monterey Bay and its environs. To watch an otter dive to the bottom of the bay and return with a sea urchin, clam, mussel, or crab on which to feed, is a joy to the eyes. More about this sentinel species and its unique habits in next week's adventure.

We Swim Together,
Tigger

Reminiscence of a Sweet Surprise (Part Two)

I ducked my head under the clear, fifty-eight-degree ocean water and came up just in time to hear a soft chirp. It must have been a call to the otter that I was babysitting because he popped his little head up and responded immediately with an excited cluck. It was mom and she was returning home to check on and feed her offspring.

Sea otters are a very chatty group and the number of their calls are not only an indication of their socially interactive lives, but a clue to their intelligence as well. They click, whistle, chirp and growl and the volume of their voices makes clear the importance of each message.

On her arrival she immediately began touching and rubbing her little one. In a matter of moments, they began to verbalize and talk to each other. Sad to say that I could not understand what they were sharing, but I got the feeling that she was asking him what he was doing with this strange human creature. No doubt the little fellow let his mom know I was a cool dude and had watched over him in her absence.

Having visited this beautiful beach many times, I have had the pleasure of observing these animated creatures in the process of dining. It begins with a roll over on the top of the water and a dive down to the bottom. It doesn't take long for an adult to return to the surface with one of their favorites. Crabs, sea urchins, abalone, clams, and mussels are the main diet for a sea otter. But wait... there's more... These furry little rascals often return to the surface with a complete dining service. They bring a flat rock up, roll over and place it on their chest as if a dinner plate. They then place the latest shell-fish delicacy on the rock and begin to crack the shell with a smaller rock, eating their meal, morsel by delicious morsel, until it is time to return to the bottom for a second round at the buffet of the Pacific.

A salt-water picnic with a baby sea otter is a wonderful memory.

Tigger

Reader's Favorites

*Thoughts that Rhyme
at Holiday Time!*

Winter | Alaskan Night

The blinding snow is behind us now
The sky begins to clear
The painting starts above us
The magic lights appear

Green as deep as emerald
Amber rich as gold
Undulate to fill the night
In His robes' great fold

In the silence of the forest
On the solar wind
I can hear his sweet clear voice
Whispering within

"May we find, in the heart of winter, the joy of nature, the beauty of the northern lights, the answer to our prayer and the warmth of Love!"

New Year's Eve | Breaking the Glass

Like snow in a globe the memories swirl
Of the year gone by
Fast the hour glass empties now
The time just seems to fly

I think of things accomplished
And those things left undone
The glory of the moments past
The battles lost and won

But tomorrow is what calls me now
This strong new voice I hear
That beckons me to come ahead
Into this brand New Year

To rise above my experience
To see things I've never seen
To step off into the mystery
And be what I've never been

So here's to our great adventures
And all that there is to see
Not what we were just yesterday
But what we were born to be

"A Blessed Happy New Year!"

The Paper

It lies stark and waiting there
A simple piece of paper bare
Plain unmarked it waits for you
To decide what you will do

Write down words inspiring power
Or like a child just draw a flower
Write your dreams compose a song
This New Year won't last too long

Paper like the day itself
Must be taken from the shelf
And there beneath the artist's hand
Draw the future make a stand

So welcome New Year fresh and bright
On your page now you must write
All the things that you *will* do
Your dreams your hopes your story true

Happy New Year!

"May all of your dreams come true!"

Valentine's Day | The Valentine

He was just a little cowboy
So he had no truck with girls
But there was one two rows ahead
With shiny golden curls
One-day he made a Valentine
And slipped it in her book
Then he watched and waited
To catch her surprised look
Her cheeks were blushed with crimson
Her smile began to grow
And now he wished he'd signed it
For she would never know
Happy Valentine's Day
I love you!

I Love You More

I love you more than an Oscar Film
Much more than a Gershwin tune
More than Winslett Jolie and Cruise
More than the man in the moon

I love you more than a good night's sleep
And the sun on a gorgeous day
I love you more than a fine dry wine
And more than a raise in pay

I love you more than a winning ticket
More than a hot poker run
More than a tip on a thoroughbred
With you I've already won

To prove how much I love you
And how you fill up my dream
I love you more than hot fudge and cherries
Yes even more than ice cream

"Now that is some kind of love...
Happy Valentine's Day!"

St. Patrick's Day | Hiding Place

Where does a leprechaun hide his gold
Where does he stash his treasure
Where does he keep his secret things
What is his deepest pleasure
Look to the hills and woodlands
Hark to the rushing glen
Look to the golden sunlight
You will have found it then

"Happy Saint Patrick's Day"

Little Men

A rustle in the underbrush
Near the rushing glen
Have ye not been warned
Beware of little men

Eyes that watch us passing
Ears that hear our tread
Hands that move our things
And leave a flower instead

Sit quietly a moment
Back against a tree
Hold your breath and just believe
And see what you shall see.

Faeries of the woodland
Won't you come out to play?
Our bigger friends have lost their smiles
And so have lost their way

Fear not these secret beings
Fear not their mischief ways
For they are the light in the forest
And protect us all of our days

"A sense of Wonder is the fountain of youth!"
Happy Saint Patrick's Day

The Circle

Standing in the circle
So many different faces
We who come together
From so many different places

Americans courageous
All so brave and free
May we have our sight restored
That we might clearly see

One another in the light
A simple place to start
Hand in hand in the beginning
Then finally heart to heart

These are precious days we share
Holy days it's true
May we allow our faith to shine
In everything we do

"A blessed Easter to all who stand in the circle."

May Day | Aloha

Aloha is the sweetest song
Of welcome home where you belong

Aloha whispers in my soul
It speaks of love complete and whole

Aloha binds us heart to heart
Friends that will not come apart

Aloha spirit fills the air
It is the very breath we share

Aloha song that never ends
It means "Until we meet again"

"I remember your dance..."

Mother's Day | Mom and Me

The best of times the worst of times
That's how it was with us
She'd praise me when I sang on key
And scold me when I'd cuss
You may have understood it
But I had to grow to see
That it was all as new to her
As it was to me
Doctors practice medicine
Mothers practice too
So blessed before you passed away
To tell you I love you

"Blessed Mother's Day"

My Mother's Eyes

Through your eyes I learned to see not just look at life
The beauty of all things around me pain and joy and strife
From you I learned the meaning of commitment to a cause
Because of you I never lost my faith in Santa Claus

Red wings in the rushes owls up in the trees
Deer out in the meadow bird songs on the breeze
Horseback in the wilderness riding without fear
It's not enough to listen you taught me how to hear

Early morning pinewood fires sharing a sunrise
Thank God I learned to see this world through my Mother's eyes

"For all of the adventures, challenges and wisdom..."
We celebrate this Mother's Day!

Memorial Day | Spirit Light and Fireflies

Tiny lights lift from the earth
And rise toward darkening skies
Their beauty reaches in my soul
And tears fill grateful eyes

Old Glory's down and folded
As night engulfs the land
The patriotic dance begins
To shine on every hand

Could it be these tiny wisps
That dance the summer night
Are spirits of the soldiers gone
Who died in freedom's fight

Rising up on golden wings
They reach toward heaven's door
Reminders of the gift they gave
At peace forevermore

"A respectful Memorial Day"

Transferring the Flag

The old man stands facing the street
His shoulders are bent, his uniform's neat
It seems the parade is passing him by
But he shares in each step and responds with a sigh

"For all of the battles won and lost
And to my fallen buddies dear Lord what a cost"
As Old Glory passes he raises his hand
And salutes the days as a much younger man

When he and the others went off to fight
For that which was true and that which was right
The little boy feels the old soldier's pride
Looks up at the tears and is touched deep inside

"Are you all right Grandpa why are you crying"
The old soldier stares at the flag a-flying:
"Boy freedom's a thing that has no ending
It needs to be cared for and it needs defending

Today you inherit the privilege to be
Courageous and brave and truthful and free
Today I'm passing this flag on to you
To do what is right and fair and what's true"

"I will Grandpa I promise," he said
And raising his little hand to his head
He gave a salute to the soldier and man
Whose bravery kept free this wonderful land

"With Blessings and Gratitude
For all Veterans"

Summer | Butterfly Shadows

Summer comes in on golden wings
And lands on the flower of time
It drinks of the nectar and shows off its color
Slowing life's rhythm and rhyme

We glance at the afternoon butterfly shadows
Then we turn back to our tasks
So much to get done and errands to run
Not hearing what summer asks

Have you slowed-down enough to hug one another
Have you watched the fireflies dance
Have you heard the laughter of children at play
Have you stopped to give summer a chance

The year is past its midpoint now
The door is closing fast
And all too soon these days will take wing
And our summertime will have passed

So now while the butterfly rests on the moment
Let us make a promise to keep
That the seeds of love will be what we sow
And joy... the harvest we reap

"Make every precious moment count...
Live, love and remember!"

Flag Day | Glory

Glory's not something that used to be
From another time and place
Glory's a feeling we hold inside
It shines on a Patriot's face
Being in love with our Nation
Not turning away when she falls
Not waiting for Her to come to us
But running to Her when she calls

*"It's Flag Day
Honor and Celebrate!"*

Father's Day | The Living Years

Have I called to tell him
Have I made it known
Without his love and guidance
I could not have grown

My first haircut, terrified
My very first romance
Life's first heartbreak whispered comfort
"Life is just a dance"

A smile replaced a tear wiped dry
A rugged hand to hold
A patient ear to hear my heart
A thousand stories told

And when one day his life is over
Looking through my tear's
Will he know how much I loved Him
In the living years

"A blessed Father's Day!"

Independence Day | Words

Behind history's door and out of our sight
Inscribed on parchment by dawn's early light
Are the words that Declare our right to be free
And the writing that Constitutes who we might be
Tonight as the fireworks light the dark sky
Do not let these precious moments slip by
But remember exactly how we came to be
The land of the brave and the home of the free

"Happy Blessed Independence Day"

Ride the Lightning

Ten nine eight seven
We count the seconds down
Soon the silver ship will fly
Unleashed from the ground

Six five four three
The colors of old glory
Unfurled in the summer breeze
Remind us of our story

Now at last two and one
As we lift-off into the sun
Freedom isn't always free
But it's what we have won

Throttle up into the blue
Into the great unknown
Courage, risk and triumph
It's how our Country's grown

So celebrate America
And hug the ones you love
Look to the sky this 4th of July
There's lightning up above

"On everyday, in every life, we are faced with events and choices that require courage. That is what it means to be an American, to Ride the Lightning!"

Autumn | Memories

The change is upon us now
Something deep inside
Hazy thoughts of yesterday
Dreams we cannot hide

Like a wondrous touching film
We see through colored glass
The lazy days of summer
The joy of summers past

This first day of autumn
A castle on the sands
A monument to memories
To life held in our hands

"Treasure fond memories and look with hope to the future!"

Labor Day | Work

Work! The way I say the word
Lets you clearly see
The way I feel about my job
And what it means to me

Whether I just spend my days
Putting in my time
Or find instead a call to serve
A worthwhile stair to climb

To recognize the lives I touch
The service I provide
This is not "work"-- it is a cause
I carry deep inside

"To each of you who through your labors
Help to make this a more prosperous world,
A restful, thankful Labor Day."

Lights Across a Field

The tractor rolls into the gathering night
The furrows lie straight and true
Folks in the city are heading home
The farmers got one row to do

Through the farmhouse window his lady appears
Her hands are covered with flour
The apple pie that awaits his return
Will sweeten their late supper hour

On the rich, brown earth of his father's land
He swings the John Deere around
And the beacon light from the window
Shines out on the fresh plowed ground

Homeward bound at the end of the day
With pride in the job we've done
As twinkling lights across a field
Replace the setting sun

"Let our service build our nation!"

A Jack-O-Lantern Moon

The mist lies in the valleys now
The crickets slow their song
The Norway maples are aflame
The leaves won't last too long

The apples crimson crisp and sweet
Hang heavy in the trees
For fruit and leaves the harvest comes
By hand or by the breeze

Darkness falls and with the dusk
A jack-o-lantern moon
Rises with the spirits
Trick or treat comes soon

And out the doorways now they come
Pirates and fairies all
Down the streets bags in hand
'Tis Halloween and fall

"Booooooo... I love Yoooooooou!"

Halloween | Fright Night

Down the lane the creatures come
Skipping hand in hand
Ghosts and goblins vampires too
They are a mighty band
While parents on the sidewalk watch
The monsters ring the bell
Princesses and Wizards
Trick-or-treat they yell
Oh that the magic of this night
Could transport little elves
Back unto a gentler time
When we felt safe ourselves

"Happy Halloween"

Secret Soldiers

He walks slowly down the street
His shoulders bend beneath the heat
He bounces grand kids on his knee
Faces he can barely see

She works in the grocery store
A clerk you know but nothing more
A homeless man a president
Angels passing heaven sent

We look but we don't realize
The story held behind those eyes
The sweet innocence of youth
Torn away in war's hard truth

You pass them by and never know
That once so very long ago
They stood to shield you from the pain
On frozen ground in jungle rain

Now when strangers come our way
May we recall this special day
And be *all that we can be*
Not just to look but really see

"With profound respect for all of the veterans of all of the wars"

Veteran's Day | The Reason

I don't like war I never have
I've seen much loss of life
Sending young ones off to fight
To face the awful strife

But as long as there are bullies
On this playground we call earth
As long as there are those who can't
Embrace what life is worth

I thank the men and women
Who take up the fight
The ones whose lives are put at risk
That we may sleep at night

"A Deeply Grateful Veteran's Day"

Thanksgiving | Homecoming

The leaves outside the window fall
Dancing red and gold
The season's past its middle age
The year is growing old

The cold wind whispers through the oak
The air is crisp and clear
The squirrel snuggles deep inside
For winter days draw near

A full moon floats above the earth
And lights the pathway home
I turn my face into the wind
And I press on alone

But summer lives within my heart
And dreams are born anew
And I give thanks for all the days
That I will share with you

"May we each bring Thanks to every day and all the whole year-long!"

Thanks Giving

Thank you for the water that soothes my deepest thirst
Thank you for the folks who the best and not the worst
Thank you for the air I breathe the earth on which I stand
Thank you for the miracle of one hinge in my hand

Thank you for my family my friends who've come to know
That our words shape the life new live they are the seeds we sow
So speak the words that heal the wounds of prejudice and hate
Replace the words the cynics choose before it is too late
Say thank you in your silence Say thank you right out loud
Say it in your deepest heart And shout it to the crowd

Thank you Lord for all these gifts for giving me the choice
For helping me to see the good and giving me a voice

"In our joyous Thanksgiving may we find the path to peace!"

Beneath a Christmas Sky

My campfire warms my hands and face
The spirit warms my soul
The coffee pot is steaming hot
A fine stew fills my bowl

My bedroll stretched out on the ground
Dry and safe and warm
While wolves howl in the distance
They mean me no harm

Bless you on these special days
May you find your heart's desire
May you live in His special ways
Beside your life's campfire

"A Merry Cowboy Christmas"

Lost and Found

Somewhere along the way we lost it
Let it slip away
Like a used up toy we tossed it
On that fateful day

Too much pretty wrapping paper
A few too many bows
One too many credit cards
Heaven only knows

No one ever bought or sold it
No one keeps it now
Distant sacred voices told it
When they taught us how

To give, to share, to really care
To find it once again
That one and only gift so rare
Sweet Love without an end

"In the spirit of the holidays, each in our own way, may we share love with our families, camaraderie with our friends, and kindness with those we meet."

Christmas | Timeless

On the floor before the fire
The cocoa warms our hands
While fragrant green and shining bright
Our Christmas pine tree stands
The Toyland myth says once you leave
You can ne'er return again
But I am proof that youth lives on
When we believe
Amen

Made in the USA
Middletown, DE
22 August 2022

71669211R00139